Trend Scope

Jonathan Lynch   Kotaro Shitori

 SEIBIDO

photographs by
Jonathan Lynch
©iStockphoto.com

音声ファイルのダウンロード／ストリーミング

CD マーク表示がある箇所は、音声を弊社 HP より無料でダウンロード／ストリーミングすることができます。下記 URL の書籍詳細ページに音声ダウンロードアイコンがございますのでそちらから自習用音声としてご活用ください。

https://seibido.co.jp/ad663

Trend Scope

はじめに

　長きにわたって実施されてきたそれまでのセンター試験に代わり、大学入学共通テストが2021年度から導入されました。どうやら、その英語の試験で受験生たちに求められたのは、限られた時間の中で必要な情報を効率よく探し出す能力、すなわち速読力のようでした。

　速読できるようになるには、英語の文章をたくさん読むことが最も重要だと考える人がいます。確かにそうした意見にも一理あるかもしれませんが、一つ一つの文章を正確に理解することのできない人が、そもそも「必要な情報を効率よく探し出す」ことができるでしょうか。目の前の一文を疎かにすることなく、そこで使用されている単語や熟語、文法事項などを丁寧に確認しながら着実に一つずつ読みこなしていく「精読」こそが、実は速読へと至る一番の近道なのではないか、精読から速読への道は常に開かれているが、その逆は必ずしもスムーズなものとは言えないのではないか、そんなことを考えながら今回私たちはこの教科書を作成しました。

　何も英語に限った話ではありませんが、物事をマスターしようとするときにまず大切なのは、基本的な知識の習得です。この始めの一歩は簡単なように見えるかもしれませんが、そこでつまずいてしまう人も実は少なくありません。英語の学習を登山に例えるなら、まずは坂道に慣れることです。そしてそのためには一定の忍耐力が必要です。もし途中で心が折れそうになったら、英語を自由自在に操っている将来の自分の姿をぜひ想像してみてください。どんなにゆっくりとしたものであっても、その歩みを止めさえしなければ、必ずいつか頂上に辿り着くことができます。

　本テキストには、「転売ヤー」「SNSの『嫌い』ボタン」「オンライン授業のハプニング」「シュリンクフレーション」「ファスト映画」「ドキシング」「ラーメンサブスク」「代替肉ハンバーガー」といった最新かつ身近で興味深いテーマが数多く取り上げられています。一人でも多くの学生さんが、このテキストを楽しみながら精読することで英語の基本をしっかり学んで、さらなる高みを目指すべく次のステップに進んでくれることを心から願っています。

　最後になりましたが、本テキストの出版に際し、成美堂編集部の小亀正人氏には大変御世話になりました。この場を借りて心より御礼申し上げます。いつも有難うございます。

Jonathan Lynch

委文　光太郎

本書の使い方

Pre-Reading Vocabulary Task

　本文中で使用されている重要な単語や熟語が選び出されています。それぞれの正しい意味を、A～J から選んでください。わからない語句でも辞書は使わず、本文中の前後の文脈から推測して答えてみましょう。

Reading Passage

　まずは、辞書を使わずに本文をひと通り読んでみましょう。それが終わったら、今度は辞書を使用して、わからない単語や熟語の意味を調べながら何度もじっくり読んでください。最後に、音声を聞きながら音読することをおすすめします。

Notes

　固有名詞や難しい語句の意味が説明されています。必要な時には参考にしてください。

Comprehension

　本文の内容が正確に理解されているかを確認するための問題です。本文の内容に合っていればTを、合っていなければFを[　　]に記入しましょう。

Summary

　本文の内容が要約できるかを確認するための問題です。下の選択肢から最も適当な語を選んでください。

Grammar Point

　本文中で使用されている重要な文法事項をわかりやすく説明しています。例文も含めてしっかりと確認しましょう。

Grammar Practice

Grammar Point で取り上げた文法事項の内容が正確に理解されているかを確認するための問題です。答え合わせをして間違っている所があれば、再度 Grammar Point に戻って確認してください。

Listening

何の準備もなくいきなり音声を聞いて空欄を埋めるやり方も可能ですが、本文の内容などを事前によく理解したうえで音声を聞くことをおすすめします。問題が難しい場合は、音声を何回も聞きましょう。また、答え合わせが済んだら、パートナーと交互に役割を替えて音読練習をしてみましょう。

Column

毎回のテーマについてさらに深く理解してもらうために、短いコラムが載せてあります。時間があれば、ぜひ読んでください。

Speaking Pairwork

まずは「会話のヒント」について学習しましょう。その後、会話モデルを使って、交互にインタビューをして、相手の答えを記入してください。

TESTUDY

本書では TESTUDY（＝ TEST ＋ STUDY）という「e-Learning ＋ オンラインテスト」システムがご利用いただけます。各 Unit の復習として、e-Learning やオンラインテストが受験できます。全て教員の指示に従って学習・受験してください。

※本サービスは教育機関におけるクラス単位でのご利用に限らせていただきます。

CONTENTS

Resellers—Good or Bad?

👥 Pre-Reading Vocabulary Task

 02

次の語は本文に出てくる重要語です。日本語の意味として最も適切なものを、A～Jから選んで（　）に記入しましょう。そして解答を確認した後、音声を聞いて覚えましょう。

1. convenient 　　（　　）　　A．商品、製品
2. product 　　　　（　　）　　B．価値のある
3. later 　　　　　（　　）　　C．後で
4. positive 　　　（　　）　　D．好ましい、肯定的な
5. negative 　　　（　　）　　E．一般の、普通の
6. opinion 　　　（　　）　　F．意見
7. profit 　　　　（　　）　　G．好ましくない、否定的な
8. ordinary 　　　（　　）　　H．便利な
9. already 　　　（　　）　　I．利益
10. valuable 　　 （　　）　　J．すでに

1 **1** Do you use the Internet for shopping? It is certainly convenient. However, on some websites, popular items are often sold out.

2 Products might be sold out because of people called **resellers**.

3 Resellers buy products at normal prices and then sell them later for
5 higher prices. They will resell anything, but popular categories for reselling are **sneakers**, **trading cards**, smartphones and toys.

4 In recent years, **more and more** people are reselling items. For some people, it is a **full-time** job and they can make a lot of money.

5 Is reselling a positive or negative thing? This is a difficult question and
10 many people have strong opinions about it.

6 Probably, most people **are against** reselling. They think that resellers buy products only to make a profit, not to use **themselves**. When ordinary people try to buy an item, it is already sold out. The only option is to pay a higher price on a **flea market app**.

15 **7** On the other hand, some people think that resellers provide a valuable service. For example, when a popular new product is sold, people **line up** outside the shop to buy it. But for most of us, lining up is impossible—we are too busy with work or school. However, if resellers line up, buy the item and then resell later, we have a chance to get the item, although the price is
20 higher of course.

8 What do you think? **Are** you **for** or against reselling?

| Notes | ....

reseller 転売屋 (ネット上では主に「転売ヤー (転売とバイヤーを掛け合わせた造語)」と呼ばれている; resell は動詞で「転売する」の意味) **sneakers** スニーカー **trading card** トレーディングカード (収集や交換を目的として作られたカード) **more and more** ますます多くの **full-time** フルタイムの、常勤の **be against** ~ ~に反対して **themselves** 彼ら自身で、自分で **flea market app** フリマアプリ (flea は「(昆虫の) ノミ」で flea market は「ノミの市」を意味する。free market (自由市場) ではないことに注意。また app は application の略語) **line up** 並ぶ **be for** ~ ~に賛成して

👥 Comprehension

本文の内容に合っていればTを、合っていなければFを[　]に記入しましょう。

1. [　　] Resellers buy items and then sell them again later.

2. [　　] Food products are popular items for reselling.

3. [　　] Reselling is part-time work only.

4. [　　] Some people dislike resellers because items become sold out.

5. [　　] Resellers give us a chance to buy items at a discount.

👥 Summary

 04

次の英文は本文の要約です。1から8の空所に、下の (a)〜(h) から適語を選んで記入し文を完成させましょう。

Resellers buy products and then sell them later for higher prices. This can be a side job or even a ❶ _____ job. Resellers can make big ❷ _____ , especially by selling goods such as sneakers. New smartphones are also ❸ _____ items for reselling. Sometimes it is ❹ _____ to buy popular items from a normal website. People must buy from resellers at ❺ _____ prices. This is one reason why people ❻ _____ resellers. ❼ _____ , resellers might be useful. For example, they line up outside a store to buy a new item. That means that we can buy the item ❽ _____ lining up, although we must pay more.

*side job：副業

(a) high	(b) however	(c) dislike	(d) popular
(e) full-time	(f) without	(g) impossible	(h) profits

🟤 Grammar Point　　　　be 動詞

☞ **be 動詞**は、基本的にふたつのものが同等であることを示すもので、「…だ、…である」と訳します。補語には 1. の名詞のほかに 2. のように形容詞を置くこともできます。

1. *This **is** a difficult question...* ［第 5 段落］ （これ＝難しい問題）

2. *... lining up **is** impossible.* ［第 7 段落］ （並ぶこと＝不可能な状態）

☞ 上記以外に「…にある、…にいる」を意味するもの (3.) や進行形 (4.)、そして受動態 (5.) を作るときにも **be 動詞**が用いられます。

3. *Your smartphone **is** on the table.*　君のスマホはそのテーブルの上にあるよ

4. *... more and more people **are** reselling items.* ［第 4 段落］

5. *... popular items **are** often sold out.* ［第 1 段落］

	主語（…は）	be 動詞（…である）	補語
肯定文	This	is	a difficult question.
否定文	This	is not (isn't)	a difficult question.
疑問文	Is	this	a difficult question?

☞ 現在形の be 動詞は主語に応じて次のように変化します。

主語			現在形	短縮形
1 人称	私	I	am	I'm
	私たち	we	are	we're
2 人称	あなた	you	are	you're
	あなたたち			
3 人称	彼 / 彼女 / それ	he / she / it	is	he's / she's / it's
	彼ら / それら	they	are	they're

🟤 Grammar Practice

A. 次の日本語に合うように英文を完成させましょう。ただし、1 つだけ余分な語があります。

1. その赤い傘は私のです。
(mine / umbrella / are / that / red / is).

....

2. 私たちの本社は東京にあります。
(Tokyo / are / our / in / head office / is).

....

3. あなたの国で留学は人気がありますか?
(in / abroad / is / studying / popular / are) your country?

....

4. 彼らはあなたの計画に反対ではありません。

(against / not / they / are / am / your) plan.

....

B. 選択肢の中で最も適切なものを選んで英文を完成させましょう。

1. The best way to solve problems ___ to work hard.
   (A) is　　**(B)** are　　**(C)** am　　**(D)** do

2. I have three brothers. One of them ___ now in London.
   (A) is　　**(B)** are　　**(C)** am　　**(D)** does

3. ___ water and light necessary for plants?
   (A) Is　　**(B)** Are　　**(C)** Am　　**(D)** Do

Listening

 05

2人の大学生が転売ヤーについて話しています。会話の音声を聞いて、空欄に聞き取った英語を書き入れましょう。そして答え合わせが済んだら、パートナーと交互に役割を替えて音読練習をしてみましょう。

Hiroshi : Hey, Susan, cool [❶　　　　　　　　] !

Susan : Thanks. I bought them from a reseller.

Hiroshi : Really? Were they expensive?

Susan : Yeah. I [❷　　　　　　　] find them in any store, so I bought them from the reseller.

Hiroshi : What do you think of reselling?

Susan : It's a difficult question! If the prices [❸　　　　　　] too high, I think it is OK. What is your opinion?

Hiroshi : I think it's a [❹　　　　　　　] . Prices become higher because of resellers.

📖 COLUMN

転売ヤーが一部で問題になっていますが、店側もただ手をこまねいているわけではありません。ある家電量販店では、人気ゲーム機を求めて並ぶ人たちに店員が購入希望の商品名を尋ねて、答えられなかった人には列から外れてもらったそうです。両者の闘いは今後もしばらく続きそうです。

まずは「会話のヒント」について学習しましょう。その後、下の会話モデルを使って、転売ヤーについて交互にインタビューをして、相手の答えを記入してください。

会話のヒント

転売ヤーについてどう思うか聞かれたら…
I think they are [good / OK / useful / not bad / not good / a problem].

その理由を聞かれたら…
Because we can buy rare items.（珍しい商品が買えるから）
　… we don't have to line up.（並ぶ必要がないから）
　… I want to be a reseller.（転売ヤーになりたいから）
　… they make prices higher.（彼らは値段を上げるから）
　… they don't use the items themselves.（彼らは自分で商品を使わないから）
　… we can't buy items at normal prices.（通常の値段では買えないから）

転売ヤーから商品を購入したことがあるかどうか聞かれたら…
Yes, I have.
No, I haven't.

A: What do you think about resellers?

B: [**Response**] ....

A: Why do you say that?

B: [**Response**] ....

A: I see. Have you ever bought an item from a reseller?

B: [**Response**] ....

A: [**If no**] OK, I see.　*[conversation is finished]*

　　or

　　[**If yes**] What did you buy?

B: [**If yes**] I bought ....

About Earphones

👥 Pre-Reading Vocabulary Task

 06

次の語は本文に出てくる重要語です。日本語の意味として最も適切なものを、A〜Jから選んで（　）に記入しましょう。そして解答を確認した後、音声を聞いて覚えましょう。

1. almost （　）　　A．幸いにも
2. heavy （　）　　B．不快な、心地よくない
3. uncomfortable （　）　　C．突然
4. suddenly （　）　　D．状況
5. painful （　）　　E．将来、未来
6. fortunately （　）　　F．理想的な
7. ideal （　）　　G．重い
8. thin （　）　　H．薄い
9. future （　）　　I．ほとんど
10. situation （　）　　J．痛い

1 **1**　Almost everybody has a nice pair of **earphones** these days. However, although the technology is excellent, sometimes earphones give us problems.

　2　For example, big **over-ear headphones** are heavy. If we wear them for a long time, they might feel uncomfortable. **Furthermore**, over-ear headphones
5 can make our ears feel hot in summer.

　3　**In-ear** Bluetooth earphones are convenient because there are no **wires,** but sometimes they might **fall out.** On a crowded train, it may be difficult to find them.

　4　In-ear earphones with wires are cheaper, but the wire may **snag on** a
10 **door handle** or bag. If the earphone **is** suddenly **pulled out of** the ear, it can feel painful.

　5　Fortunately, these problems are minor and earphones **are getting better and better**. For example, we can now buy earphones with **noise reduction**, or even **bone conduction technology**.

15 **6**　Recently, Bluetooth earphones that you can wear in bed are becoming popular. Normal earphones are not ideal for sleeping, so this new type has a soft **headband** and very thin speakers. Listening to beautiful music is a wonderful way to **fall asleep** and **ensure sweet dreams**.

　7　And in the future, earphones might get advanced AI technology and
20 start speaking to you, like a real human! You would never be lonely, and your "earphone friend" could help you with great advice for any situation.

　8　The world of earphones is exciting **for sure**, and always brings new things.

┃ Notes ┃ ⋯⋯

earphone イヤホン　**over-ear headphone** オーバーイヤー型（耳全体を覆うタイプ）のヘッドホン　**furthermore** さらに　**in-ear** インナーイヤー型（耳の中に入れるタイプ）の　**wire** ケーブル　**fall out** 抜け落ちる　**snag on ~** ～に引っかかる　**door handle** ドアの取っ手　**be pulled out of ~** ～から引き抜かれる　**be getting better and better** どんどん良くなっている　**noise reduction** ノイズリダクション（雑音低減）　**bone conduction technology** 骨伝導技術（骨を振動させることによって音を伝える技術）　**headband** ヘッドバンド、ヘアバンド　**fall asleep** 眠りに落ちる　**ensure sweet dreams** 確実に良い夢を見る（ensure は「確実にする」の意味）　**for sure** 確かに

🔬 Comprehension

本文の内容に合っていれば T を、合っていなければ F を [　] に記入しましょう。

1. [　] In the modern age, most people have earphones.

2. [　] Over-ear headphones are small-sized.

3. [　] Bluetooth in-ear earphones can fall onto the floor.

4. [　] Normal earphones are best for sleeping.

5. [　] AI "earphone friends" are now available.

🔬 Summary

 08

次の英文は本文の要約です。1 から 8 の空所に、下の (a) ～ (h) から適語を選んで記入し文を完成させましょう。

Many people ❶ _____ earphones these days. Although earphones are excellent items, there can be ❷ _____ . For example, over-ear headphones are ❸ _____ and in-ear Bluetooth earphones might fall out from our ears. However, earphones are ❹ _____ . Earphones with technology such as ❺ _____ reduction are available, and special earphones for ❻ _____ in bed are appearing, too. They can help people to fall ❼ _____ . AI technology could create earphones that talk to us like a real ❽ _____ .

(a) wearing	(b) asleep	(c) noise	(d) have
(e) improving	(f) human	(g) problems	(h) heavy

🔅 Grammar Point 　　　　　　　　一般動詞

☞ **一般動詞**には自動詞と他動詞の2種類があります。英文を読むときには、どちらの動詞として使用されているかよく確認しましょう。

1. *Almost everybody **has** a nice pair of earphones these days.* ［第 1 段落］
   ＊ この has は a nice pair of earphones という目的語をとっているので他動詞です。

2. *... but sometimes they might **fall out**.* ［第 3 段落］
   ＊ この fall out は目的語をとっていないので、自動詞の働きをする群動詞（動詞に前置詞や副詞などが付いてひとつの動詞と同じ働きをするもの）です。

自動詞	目的語をとらない	Time **passes**. 時間が過ぎる Birds **fly** in the sky. 鳥が空を飛ぶ
他動詞	目的語をとる	I **like** *English* very much. 英語がとても好きです

		主語（－は）	動詞（…する）	目的語（～を）	（修飾語句）
肯定文	［自］	He	lives		in Tokyo.
	［他］	They	play	basketball	every day.
否定文	［自］	He	does not (doesn't) live		in Tokyo.
	［他］	They	do not (don't) play	basketball	every day.
疑問文	［自］	Does he	live		in Tokyo?
	［他］	Do they	play	basketball	every day?

＊ 否定文にするときは、動詞の直前に don't / doesn't を付けて動詞を原形に戻します。
＊ 疑問文にするときは、文の頭に Do / Does を持ってきて動詞を原形に戻します。

☞ 3人称・単数・現在の -e(-es) のつけ方

普通の場合	-s をつける	like → like**s** / get → get**s** / make → make**s**
語尾が -ss, -sh, -ch, -x	-es をつける	guess → guess**es** / wash → wash**es** watch → watch**es** / relax → relax**es**
語尾が 〈子音字 + y〉	y を i に変えて es をつける	study → stud**ies** / carry → carr**ies** / fly → fl**ies**
例外	不規則な変化をする	have → ha**s** / go → go**es** / do → do**es**

🔅 Grammar Practice

A. 次の日本語に合うように英文を完成させましょう。ただし、1 つだけ余分な語があります。

1. あなたの母親はピアノを弾きますか？
(play / do / does / your / the piano / mother)?

....

2. その店は通常 8 時に閉まります。
(eight / the shop / close / usually / closes / at).

....

3. この部屋のエアコンはつきません。

The air conditioner (do / this room / work / in / does / not).

....

4. だれか好きな歌手はいますか?

(have / favorite singers / do / any / does / you)?

....

B. 選択肢の中で最も適切なものを選んで英文を完成させましょう。

1. Most of my friends ＿＿ the tennis club.
   (A) belong   (B) belongs   (C) belong to   (D) belongs to

2. My sister loves animals, but she ＿＿ to work at a zoo.
   (A) want   (B) wants   (C) don't want   (D) doesn't want

3. "＿＿ anyone want to read this comic book?"
   (A) Is   (B) Are   (C) Do   (D) Does

Listening

 09

2人の大学生がイヤホンについて話しています。会話の音声を聞いて、空欄に聞き取った英語を書き入れましょう。そして答え合わせが済んだら、パートナーと交互に役割を替えて音読練習をしてみましょう。

Miho : Alex, what kind of earphones do you have?

Alex : I have a pair of big over-ear headphones.

Miho : [❶   ] . How are they?

Alex : Great. The [❷   ] quality is excellent.

Miho : Do you ever have any problems?

Alex : Oh, sure. In the [❸   ] , my ears get hot!

Miho : Anything else?

Alex : If I use them for a long time, they feel [❹   ] .

COLUMN

WHO（世界保健機関）は、世界で約11億人の若者が、イヤホンで大音量の音楽を聞くことによって難聴のリスクにさらされていると報告しています。この種の難聴は一般に治療が困難だと言われているので、皆さんもぜひ気を付けましょう。

Speaking Pairwork

まずは「会話のヒント」について学習しましょう。その後、下の会話モデルを使って、イヤホンについて交互にインタビューをして、相手の答えを記入してください。

会話のヒント

持っているイヤホンの種類を聞かれたら …
I have [in-ear Bluetooth earphones / over-ear headphones / in-ear wired earphones（インナーイヤー型有線イヤホン）].

そのイヤホンの使用感を聞かれたら …
They are [great / excellent / good / useful / convenient].

そのイヤホンの問題点を聞かれたら …
They are heavy. / They fall out of my ears sometimes. / The wire snags on things sometimes.（ときどきケーブルが物に引っかかる）/ They make my ears hot. / Sometimes the connection is cut off.（ときどき接続が切れる）/ They break after about two years. / They are easy to lose. / The wire becomes tangled easily.（ケーブルが絡まりやすい）/ The sound quality is not good.（音質が良くない）/ Nothing in particular.（特にない）

A: What kind of earphones do you have?

B: [**Response**] ....

A: How are they?

B: [**Response**] ....

A: Do you ever have any problems?

B: [**Response**] ....

A: Anything else?

B: [**Response**] ....

Cash Registers

👥 Pre-Reading Vocabulary Task

 10

次の語句は本文に出てくる重要語句です。日本語の意味として最も適切なものを、A〜Jから選んで（　）に記入しましょう。そして解答を確認した後、音声を聞いて覚えましょう。

1. various	(　)		A. 速く
2. kind	(　)		B. さまざまな
3. customer	(　)		C. 加える、追加する
4. factor	(　)		D. 種類
5. often	(　)		E. 多くの場合、しばしば
6. quickly	(　)		F. 信頼できる
7. be worried about	(　)		G. 間違い
8. error	(　)		H. 客
9. add	(　)		I. 心配である
10. reliable	(　)		J. 要素、要因

1 **1** Shopping is very convenient these days. There are various types of **cash registers** in shops and various ways to pay.

2 Let's think about a big **home improvement store**. Sometimes, this kind of store has two types of cash registers: (1) normal registers with **store**
5 **clerks**, who **scan** items and take the customers' money; (2) **self-scan cash registers**, where we scan all items ourselves and pay using the machine (this type is called a **self-checkout** in English).

3 How can we choose the best option?

4 Speed is a big factor. Is it quicker to use the self-checkout? Often there
10 are people **lining up** at the cash registers with store clerks. Perhaps the self-checkouts are quicker. On the other hand, the store clerks **are expert at** scanning items. They can do that very quickly.

5 At the self-checkout, some people might be worried about scanning items themselves. If they make an error when scanning, they have to call a
15 member of staff. That adds more time.

6 Paying money is another aspect. For some people, it is easier to **hand over** cash or a credit card **to** a human. But these days, machines are easy and reliable, too. Young people **are good with** technology, so scanning and paying with a machine will be no problem.

20 **7** How about you? Which type do you choose?

| Notes |

cash register レジ　home improvement store ホームセンター、日曜大工店　store clerk 店員
scan ~ ~をスキャンする(商品のバーコードを読み取る)　self-scan cash register セルフスキャン
レジ　self-checkout セルフレジ　line up 並ぶ　be expert at ~ ~がうまい（expert は形容詞）
hand over A to B A を B に手渡す　be good with ~ ~の扱いに長けている

22

🔗 Comprehension

本文の内容に合っていれば T を、合っていなければ F を [　] に記入しましょう。

1. [　] Shopping is inconvenient these days.

2. [　] At a self-checkout, store clerks scan the items.

3. [　] Speed is important when choosing a cash register.

4. [　] People are worried about dropping items.

5. [　] These days, cash register machines are easy to use.

🔗 Summary

 12

次の英文は本文の要約です。1 から 8 の空所に、下の (a) 〜 (h) から適語を選んで記入し文を完成させましょう。

In some big stores, there are ❶ _____ types of cash registers. Some

cash registers have a member of staff, ❷ _____ are self-checkout

style—customers scan items ❸ _____ and pay using a machine. It

might be ❹ _____ to choose which type of register to use. Young

people are ❺ _____ with technology, so perhaps they are happy to use

a self-checkout. But some people also ❻ _____ to use a register with a

staff member. Although there may be more people ❼ _____ , the clerk

will do ❽ _____ for us.

(a) difficult	(b) good	(c) lining up	(d) different
(e) want	(f) others	(g) everything	(h) themselves

☞ **名詞**は「数えられる名詞（可算名詞）」と「数えられない名詞（不可算名詞）」に分けられます。

可算名詞	前に a/an を置く 複数形がある	I bought an **apple**. He reads many **books**.　She has two **pencils**.
不可算名詞	前に a/an は置けない 複数形はない	We went to **Yokohama**.［固有名詞］ He has much **homework**.［一定の形を持たない物質名詞］ 　water（水）/air（空気）/paper（紙）/meat（肉）など They love **music**.［抽象的な概念を表す抽象名詞］ 　kindness（親切）/advice（忠告）/information（情報）など

1. *Paying **money** is another **aspect**. For some people, it is easier to hand over **cash** or **a credit card** to **a human**.*［第6段落］
　　* money（金）と cash（現金）は不可算名詞で「一定の形を持たない物質名詞」に分類されます。
　　この2つは数えることができそうに見えますが、実際に数えるのは bill（紙幣）と coin（硬貨）
　　です。ちなみに、二重下線はすべて可算名詞です。

☞ **代名詞**は「名詞の代わりに使う言葉」で、主に同じ名詞の繰り返しを避けるために使われます。

〈人称代名詞の変化〉

人称	数	主格 （〜は、〜が）	所有格 （〜の）	目的格 （〜を、〜に）	所有代名詞 （〜のもの）	再帰代名詞 （〜自身）
1人称	単数	I	my	me	mine	myself
	複数	we	our	us	ours	ourselves
2人称	単数	you	your	you	yours	yourself
	複数					yourselves
3人称	単数	he	his	him	his	himself
		she	her	her	hers	herself
		it	its	it	—	itself
	複数	they	their	them	theirs	themselves

〈it の用法〉

① 前に出た語句を指す	She gave me a watch, but I lost **it**. 彼女に時計をもらったがなくしてしまった
② 時・天候などを表す文で使う	**It** is very hot today. 今日はとても暑い
③ 状況の it	**It** is too late. もう手遅れだ
④ 形式主語の it（to 不定詞）	**It** is easy to send an email. Eメールを送るのは簡単だ
⑤ 形式主語の it（that 節）	**It** is clear that she is crying. 彼女が泣いているのは明らかだ
⑥ かかる時間を表す文で使う	**It** takes two hours to get home. 家に着くまで2時間かかる

👥 Grammar Practice

A. 次の文に誤りがあれば訂正してください。誤りがなければ「なし」と書きましょう。

1. I bought a table and four chair in Shinjuku.

2. We did not have many rains this year.

3. Freedom is very important to us.

4. How much credit cards do you have now?

B. (   ) の中に最も適切な人称代名詞を入れて英文を完成させましょう。

1. "Whose book is this? Is this (   )?" "Yes, that's mine."

2. "Alex, this is not my homework. You should do it (   )."

3. "Good morning, kids! (   ) is time to wake up now."

👥 Listening

 13

2人の大学生が店のレジについて話しています。会話の音声を聞いて、空欄に聞き取った英語を書き入れましょう。そして答え合わせが済んだら、パートナーと交互に役割を替えて音読練習をしてみましょう。

Dylan : Hey, look, there are two types of cash registers in this [❶   ] .

Hanae : Oh, yeah. The normal type with a staff member and the self-checkout type.

Dylan : [❷   ] type do you prefer?

Hanae : I prefer the self-checkout.

Dylan : Why's that?

Hanae : I think it's [❸   ] .

Dylan : OK. [❹   ] use the self-checkout.

📖 COLUMN

今回の内容からは逸れてしまうかもしれませんが、レジで高齢者や認知症の人が慌てることなくゆっくりお金の出し入れができる「スローレジ」が、いくつかのスーパーで最近導入されています。それぞれの人の事情に合わせたレジのスタイルが今後広がるかもしれません。

まずは「会話のヒント」について学習しましょう。その後、下の会話モデルを使って、お店の
レジについて交互にインタビューをして、相手の答えを記入してください。

会話のヒント

お店のレジの好みについて聞かれたら …
I prefer [a cash register with a person / a self-checkout].
For me, [a cash register with a person / a self-checkout] is best.

選んだ理由を聞かれたら …
Because I like speaking to a person.
　　　　… the staff member does everything.
　　　　… it's easier and quicker.
Because the self-checkout is quicker.
　　　　… I like to do things for myself.
　　　　… there are few people lining up. (並んでいる人がほとんどいないから)

同じタイプのレジを毎回使うのかと聞かれたら …
Yes, always. / Yes, usually. /
Well, not always. Sometimes I might use the other type.
(いつもそうとは限らない。もう一方のレジを時々使うかもしれない)

A: In a store, what type of cash register do you prefer?

B: What do you mean?

A: I mean, do you prefer the normal type with a staff member, or do you prefer
the self-checkout?

B: I see. [**Response**] ....

A: Why's that?

B: [**Response**] ....

A: Do you always use that type?

B: [**Response**] ....

Funny Happenings During Online Lessons

Pre-Reading Vocabulary Task

 14

次の語句は本文に出てくる重要語句です。日本語の意味として最も適切なものを、A〜Jから
選んで（　）に記入しましょう。そして解答を確認した後、音声を聞いて覚えましょう。

1. accident	（　）	A. 持ち上げる
2. funny	（　）	B. 瞬間
3. as a result	（　）	C. 面白い
4. breakfast	（　）	D. 残念ながら、不運にも
5. lift	（　）	E. 費やす
6. whole	（　）	F. 会話
7. conversation	（　）	G. その結果として
8. moment	（　）	H. 朝食
9. unfortunately	（　）	I. 全体の
10. spend	（　）	J. 事故

1 **1**   Many students took online lessons during **the COVID-19 pandemic**. In fact, online lessons are still being used for some **courses**.

2   Sometimes during online lessons, accidents happen. That can be interesting! We asked a group of students in Tokyo to tell us about their 5 funny online lesson experiences.

3   Many stories were about students who forgot that their cameras were switched on. As a result, people have seen their classmates sleeping, dancing, having breakfast, **putting on makeup**, lifting **weights**, and more.

4   During online lessons, it is best to study hard and check the camera 10 **status**!

5   But it is not only the camera. Forgetting to **mute** the **microphone** can be **embarrassing**, too. Several students had done this themselves. One student was speaking to her pet dog during a lesson: "**Maron**! Maron! You're so cute! Sit here with me. I love you, Maron." The whole class including the 15 teacher could hear the conversation with Maron.

6   Teachers may have embarrassing moments, too. One student told us about a teacher who used an **animated avatar** instead of his real face at the start of the lesson. He wanted to **amuse** and **motivate** his class. **What a great teacher!** Unfortunately, he did not know how to **switch off** the avatar, so he 20 spent 90 minutes talking **in the form of** a cat.

┃ Notes ┃ ....

the COVID-19 pandemic 新型コロナウイルスの世界的流行　**course** 科目　**put on makeup** 化粧をする(put on は「身に付ける」の意味)　**weight** バーベル(鉄棒の両端に鉄盤をつけた運動用具)　**status** 状態　**mute ～** ～をミュートにする　**microphone** マイク　**embarrassing** ばつの悪い(形容詞)　**Maron** マロン(ペットの犬の名前)　**animated avatar** アニメのアバター（例えば zoom では、参加者の顔や体を動物やアニメのキャラクターに変えることができる）　**amuse ～** ～を楽しませる　**motivate ～** ～にやる気を起こさせる　**What a great teacher!**(what は感嘆用法で「なんという」の意味)　**switch off ～** ～を無効にする　**in the form of ～** ～の姿をして

🎧 Comprehension

本文の内容に合っていれば T を、合っていなければ F を [　] に記入しましょう。

1. [　] Online lessons have stopped now.

2. [　] A group of teachers told about their experiences.

3. [　] Some students have been seen dancing during lessons.

4. [　] Students' conversations have sometimes been heard, too.

5. [　] A teacher's pet cat appeared during a lesson.

🎧 Summary

 16

次の英文は本文の要約です。1 から 8 の空所に、下の (a) ～ (h) から適語を選んで記入し文を完成させましょう。

Online lessons have become ❶ _____ due to the COVID-19 pandemic.

Teachers and their students use webcams and microphones to

❷ _____ a lesson over the Internet. Occasionally, funny things happen

by ❸ _____ during these lessons. Some students may

❹ _____ to switch off their cameras. As a ❺ _____ , all the

other class members might see them eating food or exercising. Forgetting to switch

off the ❻ _____ is another problem. ❼ _____ conversations

can be heard by the whole class. Teachers have ❽ _____ moments, too.

Everybody needs to be careful!

(a) embarrassing	(b) common	(c) have	(d) forget
(e) microphone	(f) result	(g) private	(h) accident

👥 Grammar Point 　　　　過去形

☞ **過去形**は過去のある時点の動作・状態・出来事を表現するときに使用されます。

1. *Many students **took** online lessons during the COVID-19 pandemic.* [第 1 段落]
   * 過去に行われた動作を表すために took が使われています。

2. *He **wanted** to amuse and motivate his class.* [第 6 段落]

3. *Unfortunately, he **did not know** how to switch off the avatar...* [第 6 段落]
   * 2. と 3. は過去のある時期に存在した状態を表すために状態動詞の過去形が使われています。

4. *Funny things **happened** during the online lessons.*
   * 過去のある時点に起きた出来事を表すために happened が使われています。

	be 動詞 (was / were)	一般動詞
肯定文	She was busy last week.	He watched YouTube yesterday.
否定文	She was not (wasn't) busy last week.	He did not (didn't) watch YouTube yesterday.
疑問文	Was she busy last week?	Did he watch YouTube yesterday?

☞ 規則動詞の変化

	現在形	過去形
通常の動詞には語尾に -ed を付ける	help	help**ed**
語尾が -e で終わる動詞には -d を付ける	like	like**d**
語尾が〈子音字 + y〉の動詞は y を i に変えて -ed を付ける	study	stud**ied**
語尾が〈母音字 + y〉の動詞はそのまま -ed を付ける	enjoy	enjoy**ed**
語尾が〈短母音 + 子音〉の動詞は子音字を重ねて -ed を付ける	stop	stop**ped**

☞ 主な不規則動詞の変化 (現在形 → 過去形)

bring → brought	feel → felt	spend → spent	tell → told	see → saw
give → gave	go → went	put → put	drink → drank	eat → ate

👥 Grammar Practice

A. 次の日本語に合うように英文を完成させましょう。ただし、1 つだけ余分な語があります。

1. オリンピックが 2021 年に東京で行われました。
   (take / in 2021 / place / the Olympic Games / took / in Tokyo).

   ....

30

2. 彼女は子供の頃、沖縄に住んでいました。

She (when / lived / she / lives / in Okinawa / was) a child.

....

3. 昨夜は何時に寝ましたか?

(time / go to bed / what / did / do / you) last night?

....

4. 彼は先週の土曜日に友人たちと釣りを楽しみました。

He (with / enjoyed / friends / fishing / his / enjoys) last Saturday.

....

B. 選択肢の中で最も適切なものを選んで英文を完成させましょう。

1. "____ you often go to church when young?"
   (A) Do (B) Did (C) Were (D) Was

2. I waited for him for three hours but he ____ .
   (A) comes (B) came (C) doesn't come (D) didn't come

3. "Were you at today's English class?" "Yes, I ____ ."
   (A) am (B) are (C) was (D) were

Listening

 17

2人の大学生がオンライン授業について話しています。会話の音声を聞いて、空欄に聞き取った英語を書き入れましょう。そして答え合わせが済んだら、パートナーと交互に役割を替えて音読練習をしてみましょう。

Shun : Hey, Alison, have you ever had online lessons?

Alison : [❶   ], I'm still having online lessons now.

Shun : Has something funny ever happened?

Alison : During the lesson? Sure. One time my friend forgot to switch off her camera.

Shun : [❷   ] happened?

Alison : Suddenly, her pet [❸   ] jumped up onto her desk and was looking at the camera!

Shun : That's so [❹   ] !

📖 COLUMN

大学生を対象にしたあるアンケート調査によると、オンライン授業を真面目に受けていると答えた学生は約4割でした。そして他のことをしていると回答した人たちの内訳は「ゲームやスマホ44%」「他の授業の課題27%」「飲食18%」「寝ている11%」という結果でした。

👥 Speaking Pairwork

まずは「会話のヒント」について学習しましょう。その後、下の会話モデルを使って、オンライン授業について交互にインタビューをして、相手の答えを記入してください。

会話のヒント

これまでにオンライン授業を受けたことがあるかと聞かれたら …
Yes, I have. Many times. / Yes, I have. Several times. / Yes, I have. A few times. (*several times は通例 5,6 回くらいで、a few times は数回を意味します。)

何か面白いことが起きたかどうかを聞かれたら …
A classmate forgot to switch off [his/her] [camera/microphone].
We could [see/hear] [him/her] [talking/dancing/sleeping/playing a game].

面白い出来事を聞かせてもらったら …
That's so funny! / That's so interesting! / That's so cute! / That's so embarrassing!

A: Have you ever had online lessons?

B: [**Response**] ....

A: Has something funny ever happened?

B: [**Response**] ....

A: [**Reaction**] ....

B: How about you? Has something funny happened in an online lesson?

A: [**Response**] ....

B: [**Reaction**] ....

Loose-Fitting Clothing

Pre-Reading Vocabulary Task

 18

次の語は本文に出てくる重要語です。日本語の意味として最も適切なものを、A〜J から選んで（　）に記入しましょう。そして解答を確認した後、音声を聞いて覚えましょう。

1. fun	(　)	A.	現代の
2. popular	(　)	B.	季節
3. several	(　)	C.	時々
4. sometimes	(　)	D.	きつい
5. season	(　)	E.	たぶん、おそらく
6. tight	(　)	F.	平等
7. appearance	(　)	G.	楽しみ
8. perhaps	(　)	H.	外見
9. modern	(　)	I.	人気のある
10. equality	(　)	J.	いくつかの

1 **1**   Fashions are changing **all the time**. A style that **is in fashion** this year may **be out of fashion** next year. Of course, this is part of the fun of fashion. We can often see, buy and wear new styles.

2   One style has been popular for several years—**loose-fitting** clothing.
5 This style is sometimes called "**big silhouette**" in Japan. Furthermore, "**oversized**" clothing is also a loose-fitting style.

3   There are loose-fitting styles for many types of clothes: **tops**, T-shirts, **dresses**, coats and more. Every season, new loose-fitting clothes appear in the shops.

10 **4**   Why is this style so popular? We asked several young people to give us their reasons for wearing loose-fitting clothing.

5   The top reason was comfort. Loose-fitting clothes are not tight and are made from soft **materials**. If you are meeting friends in a café or just relaxing at home, casual loose-fitting clothes seem perfect.

15 **6**   Another reason was **ease of use**. One young woman said, "I don't have to think too much about my appearance when I wear loose-fitting clothes." This style is easy to wear and easy to **match with** other clothes.

7   One young man made an interesting comment. He said that this style seems to be "**unisex**." Perhaps these clothes **fit in with** modern society. **After**
20 **all**, we are **aiming for** equality between men and women.

8   **Not everybody** likes wearing tight clothing. Loose-fitting clothes are a comfortable option for young people... and also look nice!

▌ **Notes** ▌ ....

all the time 常に   **be in fashion** 流行している   **be out of fashion** すたれている   **loose-fitting**
ルーズフィットの、ゆったりした   **big silhouette** ビックシルエット (silhouette は「輪郭」の意
味)   **oversized** オーバーサイズの   **tops** トップス (上半身に着るもの)   **dress** ワンピース、ドレス
material 生地、素材   **ease of use** 使い勝手の良さ   **match with ~** ~と合う   **unisex** ユニセック
スの、男女の区別のない   **fit in with ~** ~になじむ   **after all** なにしろ…だから   **aim for ~** ~を
目指す   **not everybody** 誰もが…するわけではない (部分否定)

👥 Comprehension

本文の内容に合っていれば T を、合っていなければ F を [ ] に記入しましょう。

1. [ ] Loose-fitting clothing became popular last year.

2. [ ] Only a few types of clothes have loose-fitting styles.

3. [ ] Young people think that loose-fitting clothes are comfortable.

4. [ ] Loose-fitting clothes are easy to wear but difficult to match.

5. [ ] Both men and women can enjoy wearing loose-fitting clothes.

👥 Summary

 20

次の英文は本文の要約です。1 から 8 の空所に、下の (a) ～ (h) から適語を選んで記入し文を完成させましょう。

Although fashions ❶ _____ often, loose-fitting clothes have been in

fashion ❷ _____ . In Japan, these clothes are called "big silhouette"

or "oversized" clothes. A wide ❸ _____ of loose-fitting clothes can be

❹ _____ at fashion stores, including tops, dresses and coats. Young

people like loose-fitting clothing for ❺ _____ reasons. Many young

people say that loose-fitting clothes are very ❻ _____ . They are also

easy to wear. ❼ _____ , this style can be worn by ❽ _____

men and women.

(a) for a long time	(b) finally	(c) comfortable	(d) both
(e) change	(f) purchased	(g) several	(h) variety

🔴 Grammar Point　　進行形

☞ 現在形が〈現在の状態〉や〈現在の習慣的な動作〉を表すのに対して、**現在進行形**は〈今の時点で進行している動作〉を表します。

1. *Fashions are **changing** all the time.* [第 1 段落]

2. *If you are **meeting** friends in a café or just **relaxing** at home, casual loose-fitting clothes seem perfect.* [第 5 段落]　* just の前に you are が省略されています。

3. *After all, we are **aiming** for equality between men and women.* [第 7 段落]

☞ 以下の例文を読んで現在進行形と現在形の違いについて考えてみましょう。

4. What are you **doing** now?（現在進行形）
   * 電話や Line などで「今何しているの?」と聞くときの表現です。

5. What do you **do**?（現在形）
   * 相手が習慣的にしていることを聞くときの表現です。「何の仕事をしているの?」という意味で、What's your job? とほぼ同じです。

	現在形	現在進行形
肯定文	He **studies** English every day.	He **is studying** English now.
否定文	He doesn't **study** English every day.	He **isn't studying** English now.
疑問文	Does he **study** English every day? Yes, he does. / No, he doesn't.	**Is** he **studying** English now? Yes, he is. / No, he isn't.

☞ 過去形が〈過去の状態〉や〈過去の習慣的な動作〉を表すのに対して、**過去進行形**は〈その時 [then] 進行していた動作〉を表します。

	過去形	過去進行形
肯定文	He **studied** English yesterday.	He **was studying** English then.
否定文	He didn't **study** English yesterday.	He **wasn't studying** English then.
疑問文	Did he **study** English yesterday? Yes, he did. / No, he didn't.	**Was** he **studying** English then? Yes, he was. / No, he wasn't.

🔴 Grammar Practice

A. 次の日本語に合うように英文を完成させましょう。ただし、1 つだけ余分な語があります。

1. 私は今友人たちと昼食を食べています。
   I (lunch / am / with / eat / my friends / having) now.

   ....

2. なぜ今日はそんなに速く歩いているのですか?
   Why (you / so / are / walking / were / fast) today?

   ....

3. 今朝、雨は降っていませんでした。

(raining / rained / was / it / not / this morning).

....

4. 地震があったとき何をしていましたか?

What (you / the earthquake / did / doing / when / were) struck?

....

B. 選択肢の中で最も適切なものを選んで英文を完成させましょう。

1. "I'm sorry. Lisa can't go out now. She ____ for the test tomorrow."
   (A) studies   **(B)** studied   **(C)** is studying   **(D)** was studying

2. "Your smartphone ____ . Why don't you answer it?"
   (A) ring   **(B)** rings   **(C)** is ringing   **(D)** was ringing

3. "What ____ at ten o'clock last night?" "I was taking a bath."
   (A) do you do   **(B)** are you doing   **(C)** did you do   **(D)** were you doing

🔊 Listening

 21

2人の大学生がファッションについて話しています。会話の音声を聞いて、空欄に聞き取った英語を書き入れましょう。そして答え合わせが済んだら、パートナーと交互に役割を替えて音読練習をしてみましょう。

Jeff : Hey, Reika. I like your T-shirt. Is that [❶   ] ?

Reika : Yeah. I went shopping for clothes last [❷   ] .

Jeff : It's a loose-fitting style, right?

Reika : Yes, that's right! Do you wear loose-fitting clothes, Jeff?

Jeff : Well... yes, [❸   ] .

Reika : OK. How come?

Jeff : Because they are [❹   ] .

Reika : Yes. I agree.

📖 COLUMN

「ビックシルエット」の流行は 2017 年頃から始まったと言われていますが、それ以前は体にピッタリ合った「タイトシルエット」が 10 年くらい流行していました。そしてさらにその前は、今回と同じビックシルエットがこれまた 10 年くらいブームになっていたそうです。果たして今のこの流行も 10 年間続くのでしょうか。

Speaking Pairwork

まずは「会話のヒント」について学習しましょう。その後、下の会話モデルを使って、ルーズフィットの服について交互にインタビューをして、相手の答えを記入してください。

会話のヒント

ルーズフィットの服を着るかどうかを聞かれたら …
Yes, every day. / Yes, often. / Yes, sometimes.
No, not often. (めったに着ない) / No, never. (一度も着たことがない)

その理由を聞かれたら …
Because I like (love) them.
　　　　　 … they are comfortable.
　　　　　 … I don't like them so much.
　　　　　 … I dislike them. (嫌いだから)
　　　　　 … they don't suit me. (自分には似合わないから)

ルーズフィットの服が人気の理由を聞かれたら …
One reason is that they are unisex.
　　　　　　　 … they are easy to wear.
　　　　　　　 … they are not expensive.

A: Do you wear loose-fitting clothes?

B: [**Response**] ....

A: OK. How come?

B: [**Response**] ....

A: I see. Why are loose-fitting clothes popular, do you think?

B: [**Response**] ....

A: Sure. By the way, which shop do you recommend for buying clothes?

B: I recommend ....

Shrinkflation

🔵 Pre-Reading Vocabulary Task

 22

次の語句は本文に出てくる重要語句です。日本語の意味として最も適切なものを、A〜Jから選んで（　）に記入しましょう。そして解答を確認した後、音声を聞いて覚えましょう。

1.	happen	（　）	A.	悲しい
2.	(the) same	（　）	B.	気にする
3.	in fact	（　）	C.	高価な
4.	of course	（　）	D.	もちろん、当然
5.	expensive	（　）	E.	腹を立てて
6.	sad	（　）	F.	起こる
7.	angry	（　）	G.	気づく
8.	mind	（　）	H.	同じ
9.	decide	（　）	I.	実は
10.	notice	（　）	J.	決める

1 **1**   **Have you ever** bought a food product and thought, "**Hey**, the size has changed!"?

2   This sometimes happens. We pay the same price but the product is smaller. In fact, this situation has a special name—**shrinkflation**.

5 **3**   Of course, in most cases, we can imagine the reasons for shrinkflation. For example, the product's **ingredients** have become more expensive.

4   When a product becomes smaller, different people have different reactions. Some people might be sad. Some people might be a little angry. Other people do not mind.

10 **5**   But why does the product maker make the product smaller? A different option is to increase the price.

6   In fact, this is a problem for all **food makers** around the world. It is difficult to decide which option is best—make a smaller product or increase the price.

15 **7**   If the product is **just a little** smaller, many people may not notice. On the other hand, if there is a price increase, the product size can stay the same.

8   Which **approach** do you think is best? A smaller product for the same price or the same product for a higher price?

20 **9**   In Japan, many food products have stayed the same for many years. **Consumers** love those products and always feel happy to buy them. Perhaps food makers in Japan prefer to avoid the shrinkflation approach.

Notes

Have you ever ... ? 今までに…したことがありますか？(ever は〈経験〉を表す現在完了形とともに使用されることが多い)　**hey**（驚きや当惑などを表して）あれ、おや　**shrinkflation** シュリンクフレーション（shrink「縮む、減る」と inflation「価格上昇、インフレ」からなる造語）　**ingredient** 原材料　**food maker** 食品メーカー　**just a little** ほんの少し　**approach** 方法、取り組み　**consumer** 消費者

👥 Comprehension

本文の内容に合っていれば T を、合っていなければ F を [　] に記入しましょう。

1. [　] Shrinkflation is when a food product becomes bigger.

2. [　] Everybody becomes angry when shrinkflation happens.

3. [　] Increasing the price is one more option.

4. [　] Worldwide, all food makers have this problem.

5. [　] Shrinkflation is not an easy option for Japanese food makers.

👥 Summary

 24

次の英文は本文の要約です。1 から 8 の空所に、下の (a) 〜 (h) から適語を選んで記入し文を完成させましょう。

Sometimes, when you buy a food product, there might be a change. One

❶ _____ of change is when the food product becomes smaller. Often,

although the food product is smaller, the ❷ _____ is the same. This

is ❸ _____ shrinkflation. When this situation happens, how do you

❹ _____ ? Different people react in different ❺ _____ .

Some people do not mind. Some people do not even ❻ _____ if a

product becomes smaller. However, shrinkflation is not the only

❼ _____ for food makers. They could keep the product at the same

size and ❽ _____ the price. This approach might be more popular for

food makers in Japan.

(a) called	(b) notice	(c) increase	(d) feel
(e) ways	(f) price	(g) type	(h) option

☞ 具体的な内容について相手に聞くときは、疑問詞 (wh-, how) で始まる疑問文を使用します。Yes/No の答えを求める場合には疑問詞は使いません。

1. *But __why__ does the product maker make the product smaller?* [第 5 段落]
　* この make は「make + O + 形容詞：O を…にする」という意味の動詞です。

2. *__Which__ approach do you think is best?* [第 8 段落]
　* Which approach is best? という文に do you think（〜だと思いますか？）が挿入されています。わかりにくい場合は do you think の部分をカッコで括ってみましょう。

☞ 疑問詞の後ろは、通常の疑問文（do you 〜？や are you 〜？など）と同じです。ただし、疑問詞が主語の働きをしている場合は直後に述語動詞が来ます。

Who（誰?）	**Who** did you meet in the library? – I met my English teacher.
	Who is that boy? – He is my son.
	Who made this cake? – Kate (did).　*Who が主語の場合
What（何?）	**What** do you like for breakfast? – I like fruit.
	What happened? – There was a car accident.　*What が主語の場合
Which（どれ?）	**Which** train should I take to Shibuya?– You should take the Yamanote line.
	Which is more popular, iPhone or Android? – iPhone (is).　*Which が主語の場合
When（いつ?）	**When** is your birthday? – (It's) November 15th.
Where（どこ?）	**Where** are you from? – (I'm from) Osaka.
Why（なぜ?）	**Why** did you go to the airport? – To meet my friend.
How（どんな具合?）	**How** are you doing? – Not too bad.
（どのように?）	**How** do you get to school? – By train.
（どれくらい?）	**How** often do you check your smartphone? – Very often.

Grammar Practice

A. 次の日本語に合うように英文を完成させましょう。ただし、1 つだけ余分な語があります。

1. 誰を探しているのですか?
(looking / where / you / who / for / are) ?

....

2. どうしてそう思うのですか?
(you / why / so / makes / think / what) ?

....

3. 犬と猫ではどちらかの方が好きですか？

(do / which / you / better / what / like), dogs or cats?

....

4. 東京駅までどれくらいかかりますか？

(it / when / does / long / take / how) to get to Tokyo Station?

....

B. 選択肢の中で最も適切なものを選んで英文を完成させましょう。

1. " ___ did you buy that nice bag?" "I bought it in a shop near the station."
   (A) Why　　(B) When　　(C) Where　　(D) What

2. " ___ will your brother be back?" "He won't be back till 7 p.m."
   (A) How　　(B) Where　　(C) Why　　(D) When

3. " ___ of these YouTubers do you like best?" "Oh, sorry. I don't watch YouTube much, so I'm not sure."
   (A) Which　　(B) Who　　(C) What　　(D) How

🎧 Listening

CD 25

2 人の大学生がシュリンクフレーションについて話しています。会話の音声を聞いて、空欄に聞き取った英語を書き入れましょう。そして答え合わせが済んだら、パートナーと交互に役割を替えて音読練習をしてみましょう。

Kaori : Hey! Look! I think this chocolate bar [❶　　　　　　] become smaller.

Adam : Show me. Hey, yeah, I think it's a little smaller.

Kaori : [❷　　　　　　] too bad.

Adam : Was it cheaper? I mean, was the price lower?

Kaori : No, it was the same price. [❸　　　　　　] , I think this might be shrinkflation!

Adam : Oh, yeah! Maybe it is shrinkflation. What do you think about that?

Kaori : I don't like it but maybe it [❹　　　　　　] be helped.

📖 COLUMN

18 歳以上の男女を対象にしたある調査によると、シュリンクフレーションの事例が最近増えたと感じる、と答えた人は全体の約 7 割に上りました。そして、それを快く思わないという答えが最も多かったのは、26 歳から 35 歳までのいわゆる「ミレニアム世代」の人たちで、その数字は他の世代を大きく上回っていました。なぜこのような結果になったのでしょうか。

 **Speaking Pairwork**

まずは「会話のヒント」について学習しましょう。その後、下の会話モデルを使って、シュリンクフレーションについて交互にインタビューをして、相手の答えを記入してください。

会話のヒント

シュリンクフレーションについてどう思うか聞かれたら …
I think it's OK.
    ... it isn't good.
    ... it's terrible. (ひどいと思う)
    ... it can't be helped. (仕方ないと思う)

その理由を聞かれたら …
Because a little smaller is no problem. (少し量が減っても問題ないから)
    ... sometimes ingredient costs increase. (原材料費が上がることもあるから)
    ... I want the same size. (同じ量が欲しいから)
    ... a price increase is better. (それなら値段を高くした方がいいから)

シュリンクフレーションの例となるものを見たことがあるかどうか聞かれたら …
Yes, I have. [商品名] got smaller.
No, I haven't.

A: What do you think about shrinkflation?

B: I think ....

A: OK. Why do you say that?

B: [**Reason**] ....

A: I see. That's interesting.

B: Have you ever seen an example of shrinkflation?

A: [**Response**] ....
   How about you?

B: [**Response**] ....

🔵 Pre-Reading Vocabulary Task

 26

次の語は本文に出てくる重要語です。日本語の意味として最も適切なものを、A〜Jから選んで（　）に記入しましょう。そして解答を確認した後、音声を聞いて覚えましょう。

1. ask	（　）	A.	女性の
2. male	（　）	B.	育てる、成長する
3. environment	（　）	C.	環境
4. imagine	（　）	D.	想像する
5. view	（　）	E.	尋ねる
6. calm	（　）	F.	作物
7. female	（　）	G.	穏やかな
8. strict	（　）	H.	男性の
9. grow	（　）	I.	厳格な、厳しい
10. crop	（　）	J.	見方、意見

1 **1** In our modern world, most people live in cities or towns. Here, shops are nearby and **transportation** is available. Certainly, it is a convenient lifestyle.

2 However, recently, TV programs and YouTube videos showing
5 **countryside living** have become popular. Some people live in houses **deep in the countryside**, and their lifestyles are interesting.

3 Surprisingly, many young Japanese people like this **content**. We asked a group of college students why they liked it.

4 A male college student said that, for him, countryside living is a kind
10 of **fantasy**. He lives in an **urban** environment, but from the TV and YouTube, he can learn about a **totally** different lifestyle, and also imagine living there.

5 **What would it be like?** The students had positive views about it. They said that the lifestyle would be calm, natural, fun and full of beauty.

6 A female student talked about stress. In our lives, we have stress every
15 day, she said. However, in a house in the countryside, we could live a **stress-free** life. For example, there would be no strict **time limits** for work. If we do not finish a job by 5 p.m. today, no problem! Tomorrow is OK.

7 Another student also talked about the work. Growing crops, making things and **maintaining** the house would be the main jobs. For all of these,
20 we need to use our hands. That would be more interesting than desk work, he said.

8 Would you like to live in a house deep in the countryside?

▌ Notes ▐ ┈┈

transportation 交通機関 **countryside living** 田舎暮らし **deep in the countryside** 人里遠く離れた田舎の **content** コンテンツ（ここではテレビ番組やYouTube動画を指す） **fantasy** 幻想 **urban** 都会の **totally** 全く **What would it be like?** それはどのようなものなのでしょうか？ **stress-free** ストレスのない（名詞＋freeで「～のない」の意味） **time limit** 期限 **maintain～** ～の手入れを怠らない

🔗 Comprehension

本文の内容に合っていればTを、合っていなければFを[　]に記入しましょう。

1. [　] TV programs and videos about the countryside are not popular.

2. [　] The male student lives in the countryside.

3. [　] The students have a good image of the countryside lifestyle.

4. [　] The female student talked about being lonely.

5. [　] One student talked about the three main jobs.

🔗 Summary

 28

次の英文は本文の要約です。1から8の空所に、下の (a) ～ (h) から適語を選んで記入し文を完成させましょう。

Some people in Japan ❶ _____ in houses deep in the countryside.

TV programs and YouTube videos ❷ _____ their lifestyles. It is very

interesting content and is popular ❸ _____ young people. Some young

people like to ❹ _____ living in these houses. It would be a very

❺ _____ lifestyle, but it might have many good points. We could live

a calm life in an area of natural ❻ _____ . Also, it might be a lifestyle

without ❼ _____ . Finally, work in the countryside might be more

interesting than ❽ _____ .

(a) different	(b) beauty	(c) show	(d) desk work
(e) stress	(f) live	(g) among	(h) imagine

☞ **前置詞は**「名詞の**前**に置く詞（ことば）」という意味です。まずは、それぞれの前置詞がもつ基本的なイメージを大まかにつかんでみましょう。

1. *However, __in__ a house __in__ the countryside, we could live a stress-free life.* ［第6段落］
   * 2つの in はともに「場所」を表す前置詞です。

2. *If we do not finish a job __by__ 5 p.m. today, no problem!* ［第6段落］
   * この by は「時」を表す前置詞です。

		時		場所
at	～に	at five o'clock（時刻） at night（時）	～に［で］	**at** the post office **at** home
in	～に	**in** the morning（午前） **in** November（月） **in** 2023（年） **in** winter（季節）	～の中に［で］	**in** the box **in** bed **in** the park **in** Tokyo **in** the world
	～後に	**in** an hour（時間の経過）		
on	～に	**on** Sunday（曜日） **on** April 1（特定の日） **on** Sunday morning（特定の朝）	～の上に ～に接して	**on** the table **on** the wall
by	～までに	**by** tomorrow（期限）	～のそばに	**by** the window
for	～の間	**for** a long time	～に向かって	**for** New York
その他	～の間 ～まで（ずっと） ～から ～以来ずっと ～後に ～以内に ～よりも前に ～の間中	**during** the holidays **till [until]** recently **from** beginning to end **since** last week **after** school **within** a week **before** dark **through** the night	～へ［まで］ ～の中へ ～の下に ～の間で ～の中で ～の後ろに ～の前に ～の近くに ～を横切って	**to** the station **into** the room **under** the bridge **between** you and me **among** young people **behind** the door **in front of** the shop **near** here **across** the street

👥 **Grammar Practice**

A. 次の日本語に合うように英文を完成させましょう。

1. 私の両親は7月15日の午前にパリに到着するでしょう。
   My parents (in / the morning / arrive / on / will / Paris) of July 15.

   ....

2. 彼は博多から東京までバスに乗りました。
   He (from / took / to / Hakata / a bus / Tokyo).

   ....

3. 私はたいてい土曜日は午前 1 時に寝ます。

I usually (on / bed / to / at / go / 1 a.m.) Saturdays.

....

4. 彼女は夏の間に 1 週間入院しました。

She (the hospital / was / for / in / during / one week) the summer.

....

B. 選択肢の中で最も適切なものを選んで英文を完成させましょう。

1. The teacher is very popular ___ the students.

   (A) in   **(B)** between   **(C)** among   **(D)** for

2. We must get to the station ___ 6 a.m. tomorrow.

   (A) by   **(B)** till   **(C)** within   **(D)** since

3. "I'm busy now. Can you call me ___ ten minutes?"

   (A) in   **(B)** for   **(C)** by   **(D)** through

🔊 Listening

 29

2 人の大学生が田舎暮らしについて話しています。会話の音声を聞いて、空欄に聞き取った英語を書き入れましょう。そして答え合わせが済んだら、パートナーと交互に役割を替えて音読練習をしてみましょう。

Graham : Hey, Yukiko, what do you think about living deep in the countryside?

Yukiko : I think it's good. I sometimes watch TV programs about it.

Graham : [**❶**   ]? Would you like to live there?

Yukiko : [**❷**   ] !

Graham : How come?

Yukiko : I love nature. It would be [**❸**   ] to live in the middle of such wonderful nature.

Graham : Yeah. That's for [**❹**   ] !

📖 COLUMN

田舎暮らしを実行する前にやるべきこととして、次の 3 点がある不動産会社のサイトで紹介されていました。興味がある人は参考にしてください。
① 移住を希望するエリアのことをよく調べること
② 移住後の収入と支出をシミュレーションすること
③ 取りあえず短期滞在してみること

Speaking Pairwork

まずは「会話のヒント」について学習しましょう。その後、下の会話モデルを使って、田舎暮らしについて交互にインタビューをして、相手の答えを記入してください。

会話のヒント

テレビや YouTube で田舎暮らしのコンテンツを見るか聞かれたら …
Yes, often. / Yes, sometimes.
No, not often.（めったに見ない）/ No, never.

人里遠く離れた田舎の家に住んでみたいかと聞かれたら …
Yes, I would. Very much! / Yes, maybe I would. / I'm not sure.（わからない）/
Maybe I wouldn't. / No, I wouldn't. No way!（絶対嫌だ）

その理由を聞かれたら …
It would be [fun / interesting / calm / peaceful / lonely / scary（怖い）/
                depressing（気がめいる）].
We could enjoy [beautiful nature / clean air / wonderful views /
                the four seasons（四季）].
The lifestyle would be [fun / unique / rewarding（価値のある）/ tough（きつい）/
                exhausting（とても疲れる）].
I would miss [the urban environment / shops / nightlife（夜遊び）/ my friends].
The work would be [interesting / stress-free / practical（実際的な）/ tiring（疲
                れる）/ difficult].

A: Do you watch content about countryside living on TV or YouTube?

B: [**Response**] ....

A: Would you like to live in a house deep in the countryside?

B: [**Response**] ....

A: How come?

B: [**Response**] ....

A: I see. Anything else?

B: [**Response**] ....

UNIT 8

Hanging Out in Streets and Parks

🎵 Pre-Reading Vocabulary Task

 30

次の語は本文に出てくる重要語です。日本語の意味として最も適切なものを、A～Jから選んで（　）に記入しましょう。そして解答を確認した後、音声を聞いて覚えましょう。

1. early （　）　　A. 雰囲気
2. park （　）　　B. 公園
3. normally （　）　　C. 味わう、楽しむ
4. still （　）　　D. 言及する
5. atmosphere （　）　　E. 早く
6. casual （　）　　F. 普通に
7. weather （　）　　G. 近くの
8. mention （　）　　H. 気楽な、形式ばらない
9. nearby （　）　　I. 今でも、まだ
10. enjoy （　）　　J. 天気

1 **1** During **the COVID-19 pandemic**, many restaurants and other places were closed. Even some coffee shops closed early. It was hard, especially for young college students, who had no places to **hang out** with friends.

2 **At that time**, meeting outside became a popular option. We often saw
5 groups of young people hanging out in parks near their colleges, or meeting on streets in popular areas.

3 Now there is an interesting thing. Although restaurants and bars are opening normally, some young people still meet outside! It seems to be a popular option, especially **from** spring **to** autumn.

10 **4** What are the reasons for this? We asked some young college students in Tokyo why they still do it.

5 Some people said that they like the atmosphere. It seems casual and **friendly** to meet outside. And if the weather is nice, it feels good to be outside in the evening.

15 **6** Other young people mentioned the cost. If the friends meet outside, the cost is **much** lower than a restaurant. For example, everyone can buy drinks and snacks at a nearby convenience store.

7 One young person said that he loves convenience store **food products**... especially cakes. Meeting outside is a chance to enjoy those delicious items
20 with friends. "But, of course, I take my **litter** home," he added.

8 How about you? Do you hang out outside?

| Notes |

the COVID-19 pandemic 新型コロナウイルスの世界的流行 **hang out** ぶらぶら時間を過ごす、たむろする **at that time** 当時 **from A to B** AからBまで **friendly** 居心地のよい（形容詞） **much** （比較級の前に置いて）はるかに、ずっと **food product** 食品 **litter** ごみ

🔣 Comprehension

本文の内容に合っていればＴを、合っていなければＦを [　] に記入しましょう。

1. [　] Many restaurants were closed during the pandemic.

2. [　] During the pandemic, meeting indoors was a popular option.

3. [　] Winter is the most popular time for meeting outdoors.

4. [　] If young people meet outdoors, they can save money.

5. [　] The young man loves to buy sweet things at convenience stores.

🔣 Summary

 32

次の英文は本文の要約です。１から８の空所に、下の (a) ～ (h) から適語を選んで記入し文を完成させましょう。

The COVID-19 pandemic was a ❶ _____ time for many people. Many places were ❷ _____ , so young people could not meet at restaurants or cafés, for example. ❸ _____ , young people started to meet friends outside. Groups would get together in parks or on streets, ❹ _____ in the evening. But even now, when restaurants are opening ❺ _____ , some young people still meet outside. One ❻ _____ for this is the casual atmosphere. Another reason is cost. It is much ❼ _____ to meet outside than in a restaurant. Finally, the members can ❽ _____ delicious food from convenience stores.

(a) reason	(b) closed	(c) instead	(d) enjoy
(e) hard	(f) especially	(g) cheaper	(h) normally

☞ **接続詞** は「語句と語句」や「節と節」をつなぐ（接続する）もので、and などの等位接続詞と because のような従属接続詞があります。

1. *We often saw groups of young people hanging out in parks near their colleges, __or__ meeting on streets in popular areas.* [第 2 段落]
   * or は hanging out ～ colleges と meeting on ～ areas を結びつけています。

2. ___Although___ *restaurants and bars are opening normally, some young people still meet outside!* [第 3 段落]
   * although (though) は「…だけれども」の意味で「譲歩」を表します。although は though よりもかたい表現です。

3. *... __if__ the weather is nice, it feels good to be outside in the evening.* [第 5 段落]
   * if は「もし…ならば、仮に…だとすれば」の意味で「仮定」や「条件」を表します。

等位接続詞 （語句と語句、節と節を対等な関係で結びつけます）	
and(A と B)	I can play <u>the piano</u> **and** <u>the guitar</u>. ピアノとギターが弾けます The sun <u>rises in the east</u> **and** <u>sets in the west</u>. 太陽は東から出て西に沈む
or(A または B)	Shall I <u>call you</u>, **or** <u>email you</u>? 電話しましょうか、それともメールしましょうか
but(しかし)	<u>I didn't want to study</u>, **but** <u>I had to</u>. 勉強したくなかったが、しなければならなかった
so(だから)	<u>I was sick</u>, **so** <u>I couldn't go to school</u>. 病気だったので学校に行けなかった

* 2つの下線部がそれぞれの等位接続詞によって結びつけられています。

従属接続詞 （従属節 [従属接続詞で始まる節] を主節 [もう一方の節] に結びつけます）	
when(～するとき)	<u>It is cold</u> **when** it snows. 雪が降るときは寒い
if(～ならば)	**If** I need your help, <u>I will call you</u>. あなたの助けが必要なら電話します
because(～なので)	<u>He didn't come</u> **because** he was busy. 忙しかったので彼は来なかった
although(～だけれども)	**Although** it was expensive, <u>I bought it</u>. 高かったけれどそれを買った

* 下線部が主節です。そして、上のすべての例文の主節と従属節は入れ替えることができます。
  例) It is cold when it snows. ⇄ When it snows, it is cold.

Grammar Practice

A. 文の順番は変えずに文と文の間に最も適当な接続詞を入れて一つの文にしましょう。

1. I went to the library yesterday.　It was closed.

   ....

2. She couldn't get up early in the morning.　She was late for school.

   ....

3. He ate lunch quickly in the cafeteria. He was very hungry.

....

4. Shall we go for a walk? Would you like to stay at home?

....

B. 選択肢の中で最も適切なものを選んで英文を完成させましょう。

1. The shop buys ＿＿ sells used books.
   (A) and   **(B)** for   **(C)** but   **(D)** so

2. ＿＿ it rains tomorrow, the baseball game will be cancelled.
   (A) When   **(B)** Because   **(C)** Although   **(D)** If

3. ＿＿ she was very tired, she finished her homework before going to bed.
   (A) When   **(B)** Because   **(C)** Although   **(D)** If

🎧 Listening

🎵 CD 33

2 人の大学生が友達と過ごす場所について話しています。会話の音声を聞いて、空欄に聞き取っ
た英語を書き入れましょう。そして答え合わせが済んだら、パートナーと交互に役割を替えて
音読練習をしてみましょう。

Maki : Hey, Trent, do you hang out outside?

Trent : You mean... in the [**❶**   ] ?

Maki : Yeah. Do you meet your friends outside?

Trent : Sure. We hang out in the square near the [**❷**   ] .

Maki : Why do you meet like that?

Trent : Well... if the weather is [**❸**   ] , it feels good. Also, there's no
need to make a restaurant reservation!

Maki : I see... that's a good [**❹**   ] !

📖 COLUMN

特に夏の涼しい夜などは公園で過ごすと快適ですが、危険なこともあります。友人たちと
公園にいたら、「ここでゴミ拾いをしているインカレのボランティアサークルです」と声
をかけられ、その後、怪しいセミナーに誘われたという事例が複数報告されているそうで
す。くれぐれも注意しましょう。

Speaking Pairwork

まずは「会話のヒント」について学習しましょう。その後、下の会話モデルを使って、友達と過ごす場所について交互にインタビューをして、相手の答えを記入してください。

会話のヒント

友達と外でぶらぶら時間を過ごすか聞かれたら …
Yes, I do. I hang out with friends [in the park / near the station / downtown(繁華街で)]. / No, I don't.

その理由を聞かれたら …
It feels good. / The cost is low. / We feel free. / It's casual. / We enjoy convenience store food.
It's too cold. / I prefer indoors. / I don't like eating outside. / It might be dangerous.

外で会うことの良い点を聞かれたら …
The cost is low. / It's lively.(にぎやかなところ) / We don't have to reserve a restaurant.(飲食店を予約する必要がない) / It feels good.

悪い点を聞かれたら …
The group might become too noisy.(集まった人たちがとても騒がしくなるかもしれない)
Some people drop litter. （ごみを捨てる人がいる）
There might be no toilet nearby. （近くにトイレがないかもしれない）

A: Do you hang out outside with friends?

B: [**Response**] ....

A: Why is that?

B: [**Response**] ....

A: What is a good point about meeting outside?

B: [**Response**] ....

A: OK. What is a bad point?

B: [**Response**] ....

Plant Burgers Are Popular in America

🔵 Pre-Reading Vocabulary Task

CD 34

次の語は本文に出てくる重要語です。日本語の意味として最も適切なものを、A～Jから選んで（　）に記入しましょう。そして解答を確認した後、音声を聞いて覚えましょう。

1. strange	（　）	A．	不思議な、奇妙な
2. however	（　）	B．	味
3. contain	（　）	C．	しかしながら
4. instead	（　）	D．	～の方を好む
5. taste	（　）	E．	その代わりに
6. identify	（　）	F．	天然の、自然の
7. challenge	（　）	G．	含む
8. prefer	（　）	H．	科学者
9. natural	（　）	I．	難問、挑戦
10. scientist	（　）	J．	識別する、特定する

1 **1** Do you like eating meat? For many young people, a hamburger with a **juicy** beef **patty** is a popular **food item**.

2 But do we eat too much meat? Some people think so. For health reasons, perhaps we should eat more vegetables and less meat.

5 **3** It seems strange but, in America, hamburger restaurants are helping people to eat less meat. These days, most **burger chains** have **plant-based** burgers on the **menu**, and these are becoming popular.

4 Plant-based burger patties look like real burgers. However, they contain no meat. Instead they are made from **pea** protein, **soy** protein or
10 other **plant proteins**.

5 The big question is about taste. If people do a **blind tasting test**, can they identify the real burger and the plant-based one?

6 People are trying this challenge, and uploading their **videos** to the Internet. In most cases, people can **tell** which burger is meat and which is
15 plant.

7 But there is an interesting thing. Before they know the true result, some people say that they prefer the taste of the plant-based burger!

8 **Food technology** has improved **a lot**. Using natural plant **ingredients**, scientists can make food that looks like meat and tastes good.

20 **9** Burger chains in Japan are already selling plant-based burgers. Have you tried one **yet**?

Notes

juicy ジューシーな、肉汁たっぷりの　patty パティ(挽肉などを円形に薄く成型したもの)　food item 食べ物(item は「品目」の意味)　burger chain ハンバーガーチェーン店　plant-based 植物をベースに作られた　menu メニュー　pea エンドウ豆　soy 大豆(=soybean)　plant protein 植物性蛋白質　blind tasting test 目隠しの味覚テスト (何のハンバーガーかを知らせずに食べて当ててもらう)　video 動画　tell ~ ~を見分ける　food technology 食品技術　a lot 大いに　ingredient 原料　yet (疑問文で) もう

🔵 Comprehension

本文の内容に合っていればＴを、合っていなければＦを [　] に記入しましょう。

1. [　] Hamburgers are popular among many young people.

2. [　] Burger chains in America are offering plant-based burgers.

3. [　] Plant-based burgers might contain soy protein.

4. [　] Meat burgers and plant-based burgers taste exactly the same.

5. [　] Plant-based burgers are not sold in Japan.

🔵 Summary

 36

次の英文は本文の要約です。１から８の空所に、下の (a) ～ (h) から適語を選んで記入し文を完成させましょう。

Eating a juicy beef hamburger sometimes is no ❶＿＿＿＿＿＿＿＿ , but some

people might eat too much meat. For them, plant burgers might be a good

❷＿＿＿＿＿＿＿＿ . In America, these burgers have become ❸＿＿＿＿＿＿＿＿

recently. They are ❹＿＿＿＿＿＿＿＿ from plant proteins. Thanks to new food

technology, the ❺＿＿＿＿＿＿＿＿ of plant-based burgers is good. In fact,

some people ❻＿＿＿＿＿＿＿＿ plant burgers to meat burgers. There are some

"plant-burger-❼＿＿＿＿＿＿＿＿-meat-burger" videos on the Internet! The

❽＿＿＿＿＿＿＿＿ of the people are interesting. Plant-based burgers are also

available in Japan.

(a) made	(b) taste	(c) idea	(d) versus
(e) problem	(f) reactions	(g) prefer	(h) popular

*A versus B : A 対 B

☞ **現在完了形**は「have [has] +過去分詞」の形で「完了」「結果」「経験」「継続」を表します。
　この形が使われていると、過去の出来事が何らかの形で現在まで繋がっていることを意味します。

1. *Food technology **has improved** a lot.* [第8段落]　＊完了を表す現在完了形です。

2. ***Have** you **tried** one yet*? [第9段落]　＊完了を表す現在完了形です。

☞ 現在完了形の作り方

肯定文	主語 + have/has + 過去分詞 …	I have eaten fish and chips.
否定文	主語 + have/has + not + 過去分詞 …	I have not (haven't) eaten fish and chips.
疑問文	Have/Has + 主語 + 過去分詞 … ?	Have you eaten fish and chips?

☞ 現在完了形の意味

意味	よく一緒に使われる語	例文
完了	already, yet など	I **have** just **finished** breakfast. 朝食を食べ終えたばかりだ
結果	already, yet など	He **hasn't spent** all his money yet.　＊not ~ yet：まだ~ない 彼はまだお金を全部使っていない → 今まだお金が残っている
経験	never, before など	**Have** you ever **visited** Kyoto? 今までに京都を訪れたことがありますか？
継続	since, for など	I **have lived** here since 2010. 私は2010年からここに住んでいる

☞ 現在完了形と過去形の違い

＊明確な過去を表す語句（ago, yesterday, last year, then, when など）があると、現在完了
　形は使えませんが、since の後ろに yesterday や last year, then などを置けば使用できます。

[O] I met you yesterday.	[×] I have met you yesterday.
[O] I watched the movie when I was a child.	[×] I have watched the movie when I was a child.
[O] I was in the hospital then.	[×] I have been in the hospital then.
[O] I haven't seen her since then.	[×] I didn't see her since then.

☞ have/has の短縮形

I have ⇒ **I've**　He has ⇒ **He's**　It has ⇒ **It's**　have not ⇒ **haven't**　has not ⇒ **hasn't**

A. 次の日本語に合うように英文を完成させましょう。

1. 私は以前にギリシャ料理を食べたことがありません。
　(never / have / Greek food / eaten / I / before).

　...

2. 今までにアイルランドに行ったことはありますか?

(ever / you / to / been / have / Ireland)?

....

3. 彼女は (彼が) 赤ん坊のときから彼を知っています。

She (since / known / was / him / has / he) a baby.

....

4. どのくらい長く英語を勉強していますか?

(long / been / you / have / studying / how) English?

....

B. 選択肢の中で最も適切なものを選んで英文を完成させましょう。

1. I ＿＿ my homework, so I can go to karaoke now.

   (A) finish　　**(B)** don't finish　　**(C)** have finished　　**(D)** haven't finished

2. There ＿＿ a big earthquake in Japan in 2011.

   (A) is　　　**(B)** has been　　**(C)** was　　　**(D)** has

3. My brother ＿＿ back from studying abroad a few days ago.

   (A) came　　**(B)** has come　　**(C)** comes　　**(D)** hasn't come

🎧 Listening

 37

2 人の大学生が植物をベースにしたハンバーガーについて話しています。会話の音声を聞いて、空欄に聞き取った英語を書き入れましょう。そして答え合わせが済んだら、パートナーと交互に役割を替えて音読練習をしてみましょう。

Kazuki : Paula, do you eat hamburgers?

Paula　: Sure! I love them. I had one [❶   ] , in fact.

Kazuki : Why do you like them so much?

Paula　: Well, I like the [❷   ] , of course. Also, they're fun and not
[❸   ] .

Kazuki : What do you think of plant-based burgers?

Paula　: I think they might be good. They might be [❹   ] .

Kazuki : Yeah, and I heard they can be delicious.

📖 COLUMN

代替肉のハンバーガーには、本文で取り上げた大豆などの植物性蛋白質からなるものと、動物の細胞を体外で培養した培養肉の2種類があります。現段階では世界的に見ても植物性の方が多く流通しているようですが、将来的には培養肉のシェアが拡大していくことが予想されています。

Speaking Pairwork

まずは「会話のヒント」について学習しましょう。その後、下の会話モデルを使って、植物をベースにしたハンバーガーについて交互にインタビューをして、相手の答えを記入してください。

> **会話のヒント**
>
> ハンバーガーを食べるかと聞かれたら …
> Yes, often. / Yes, sometimes. / Well, not so often. /
> No, hardly ever.（めったに食べない）/ No, never.
>
> 植物をベースにしたハンバーガーについてどう思うか聞かれたら …
> I think they are a good idea. / I don't think they are a good idea.
>
> その理由を聞かれたら …
> They might be healthy. / They might taste good. / They might be more
> expensive. / They might taste bad.
>
> メニューにそのハンバーガーがあったら食べるかと聞かれたら …
> Yes, I would. / Well, I might. / I'm not sure.（わからない）/ No, I wouldn't.

A: Do you eat hamburgers?

B: [**Response**] ....

A: What do you think of plant-based burgers?

B: [**Response**] ....

A: Why do you say that?

B: [**Response**] ....

A: Would you eat a plant-based burger, if you saw one on the menu in a fast
food restaurant?

B: [**Response**] ....

UNIT 10 South Korean Culture Is Popular Worldwide

👥 Pre-Reading Vocabulary Task

 38

次の語は本文に出てくる重要語です。日本語の意味として最も適切なものを、A～Jから選んで（ ）に記入しましょう。そして解答を確認した後、音声を聞いて覚えましょう。

1. wear	( )	A．服
2. clothes	( )	B．得る
3. other	( )	C．他の
4. aspect	( )	D．賞
5. dish	( )	E．優れた
6. gain	( )	F．側面
7. attention	( )	G．着る
8. famous	( )	H．料理、皿
9. award	( )	I．有名な
10. excellent	( )	J．注目

1 **1** South Korean culture is popular around the world. Many young people love South Korean bands such as **BTS**, **EXO**, **BLACKPINK** and **TWICE**, and also like to wear South Korean-style clothes.

2 But it is not only music and fashion. Other aspects of South Korean
5 culture are popular, too.

3 For example, Korean food has **become a big hit** in Tokyo. Many young people visit Shin Okubo to try out **lively** Korean restaurants. Dishes such as **samgyeopsal** and **cheese dak-galbi** are delicious and fun to eat.

4 South Korean movies and TV series have gained attention. **"Parasite"**
10 was a famous **black comedy** that won several awards. On Netflix, the South Korean TV series **"Squid Game"** became a big hit, especially among young people. It was a dark and shocking story, but with excellent **acting** from **the cast**.

5 When did South Korean culture first become **globally** popular?
15 Perhaps it started in 2012 with the song **"Gangnam Style"** by South Korean rapper **Psy**. This unique song became a hit on YouTube and got more than 4 **billion views**!

6 Many young people like South Korean music because it seems fresh. The pop stars are attractive and trendy. When they perform, they have a lot
20 of energy and their songs are **catchy**.

7 Due to the COVID-19 pandemic, it has been difficult to travel abroad. But surely, when travel returns to normal, many young people will visit Korea and enjoy Korean culture **firsthand**.

| Notes |

BTS ビーティーエス（7人組の男性ヒップホップグループ）　**EXO** エクソ（9人組の男性アイドルグループ）　**BLACKPINK** ブラックピンク（4人組の女性アイドルグループ）　**TWICE** トワイス（9人組の女性アイドルグループ）　**become a big hit** 一大ブームになる　**lively** にぎやかな　**samgyeopsal** サムギョプサル（豚バラ肉を焼いた料理）　**cheese dak-galbi** チーズタッカルビ（鶏肉と野菜を甘辛く炒めてチーズを加えた料理）　**"Parasite"**『パラサイト』（2019年公開の映画）　**black comedy** ブラックコメディー（ブラックユーモアを交えたコメディー）　**"Squid Game"**『イカゲーム』（2021年配信のドラマ）　**acting** 演技　**the cast** 出演者全員　**globally** 世界的に　**"Gangnam Style"**『江南スタイル』　**Psy** サイ　**billion** 10億　**view** 再生回数、視聴回数　**catchy** 覚えやすい　**firsthand** じかに、直接

Comprehension

本文の内容に合っていれば T を、合っていなければ F を [　] に記入しましょう。

1. [　] South Korean music is more popular than South Korean fashion.

2. [　] Young people in Tokyo like Korean restaurants.

3. [　] "Squid Game" was very popular among young people.

4. [　] The song "Gangnam Style" was a hit in 2012.

5. [　] Many people visited South Korea during the COVID-19 pandemic.

Summary

 40

次の英文は本文の要約です。1 から 8 の空所に、下の (a) ～ (h) から適語を選んで記入し文を完成させましょう。

Young people ❶＿＿＿＿＿＿＿ the world like South Korean culture. Famous

pop groups from South Korea have many ❷＿＿＿＿＿＿＿ in many countries.

In addition, South Korean food culture is ❸＿＿＿＿＿＿＿ to many places. An

area in Tokyo called Shin Okubo has many Korean restaurants. It is often crowded

with young people enjoying Korean ❹＿＿＿＿＿＿＿ . Movies and TV series

from South Korea are also ❺＿＿＿＿＿＿＿ . They have won

❻＿＿＿＿＿＿＿ . A ❼＿＿＿＿＿＿＿ called Psy might be the man who

made South Korean culture world-famous. His song "Gangnam Style"

❽＿＿＿＿＿＿＿ a big hit on YouTube.

| (a) became | (b) dishes | (c) awards | (d) popular |
| (e) fans | (f) rapper | (g) spreading | (h) around |

☞ 未来を表す表現には〈**will** ＋動詞の原形〉と〈**be going to** ＋動詞の原形〉があります。この2つの表現には共通する点と異なる点があるので注意しましょう。

1. *But surely, when travel returns to normal, many young people __will__ visit Korea and enjoy Korean culture firsthand.*　[第 7 段落]

　　* 文中の will は「時間が経過すれば自然にそうなるだろう」という「単純な未来の予想（単純未来）」を表します。

単純な未来の予想 **will**（〜だろう） **be going to**（〜しそうだ）	It **will** rain tomorrow. 明日は雨が降るだろう It **is going to** rain tomorrow. 明日は雨が降りそうだ［主観的判断］ * 基本的に2つの文の意味はほぼ同じですが、will は単なる予測で、be going to は何らかの兆候に基づいた予測です。
強い意思 **will**（〜するつもりだ）	I **will** do my best. 最善を尽くすつもりだ
意思・計画 **be going to** （〜するつもりだ）	I **am going to** buy a new smartphone today. 私は今日新しいスマートフォンを買うつもりだ * 前もって決めていたことを表すときに使います。

☞ will と be going to の違い

will：話をしている場で急にそうする気になったことを表します。
"This suitcase is very heavy. Can you give me a hand?" "OK, I **will** help you." 「このスーツケースとても重いの。手を貸してもらえます?」「いいですよ、手伝いますよ。」
be going to：話をする以前からそうするつもりでいたことを表します。
"How about going to the café now?" "Sorry, I **am going to** study for the test." 「今からカフェに行かない?」「ごめんなさい。テストの勉強をする予定なんです。」

☞ その他の未来表現

現在進行形〈be + ~ing〉	I **am moving** to Kobe next month. 来月神戸に引っ越します * 近い未来の予定を表すことができます。

🔴🔴 **Grammar Practice**

A. 次の日本語に合うように英文を完成させましょう。ただし、1つだけ余分な語があります。

1. 明日何をする予定ですか?

　(are / going to / what / you / will / do) tomorrow?

　..

2. 私は自分の夢を決してあきらめません。

　I (give / will / never / up / am going to / my dream).

　..

3. 私たちはその計画を変えないつもりです。

We (to / change / not / are / will / going) the plan.

....

4. 彼は今月の終わりにここを出て行きます。

He (at / leaving / here / the end / is / will) of this month.

....

B. 選択肢の中で最も適切なものを選んで英文を完成させましょう。

1. "Look at the black clouds in the sky. It ___ rain soon."

   (A) will   **(B)** won't   **(C)** is going to   **(D)** isn't going to

2. "The telephone is ringing, but I can't answer it now." "Don't worry. I ___ get it."

   (A) will   **(B)** won't   **(C)** am going to   **(D)** am not going to

3. Today is my mother's birthday. I ___ write a letter to her.

   (A) will   **(B)** won't   **(C)** am going to   **(D)** am not going to

🎧 Listening

 41

2 人の大学生が韓国の文化について話しています。会話の音声を聞いて、空欄に聞き取った英語を書き入れましょう。そして答え合わせが済んだら、パートナーと交互に役割を替えて音読練習をしてみましょう。

Rebecca ： Masato, which South Korean bands do you like?

Masato ： Good [❶   ]! I like BTS and TWICE.

Rebecca ： Really? Why do you like them?

Masato ： Their music is [❷   ] and they look [❸   ].

Rebecca ： How about Korean food?

Masato ： I love it! Especially bibimbap.

Rebecca ： Hey, [❹   ] go to a Korean restaurant soon!

Masato ： Great idea!

📖 COLUMN

コロナの影響で海外に行きたくても行けない若者たちの間で、韓国料理や韓国のアイテムを部屋中に並べて、韓国旅行をしているかのような写真を SNS に投稿する「渡韓ごっこ」が一時期流行りました。そしてこれに便乗して、「渡韓ごっこプラン」を提供する国内のホテルも現れました。

Speaking Pairwork

まずは「会話のヒント」について学習しましょう。その後、下の会話モデルを使って、韓国の文化について交互にインタビューをして、相手の答えを記入してください。

> ### 会話のヒント
>
> どの韓国のグループが好きかと聞かれたら …
> I like 〜 . / My favorite band is 〜 . / I am into 〜 . (私は〜に夢中だ)
>
> その理由を聞かれたら …
> Their music is [great / cool / lively (陽気な)].
> Their songs are [good / catchy (覚えやすい) / interesting].
> They look [nice / trendy (おしゃれに) / fresh].
> Their dancing is [cool / energetic / amazing].
>
> 韓国の食べ物は好きかと聞かれたら …
> I love it. / I like it. / It's OK. / It's a little hot and spicy for me.
>
> 韓国料理屋に行こうと誘われたら …
> Great idea! / Let's do it! / I'd love to! (ぜひとも) / Sure! (もちろん)

A: Which South Korean bands do you like?

B: [**Response**] ....

A: Really? Why do you like them?

B: [**Response**] ....

A: I see. How about Korean food?

B: [**Response**] ....

A: Hey, let's go to a Korean restaurant soon!

B: [**Response**] ....

Doxing

👥 Pre-Reading Vocabulary Task

🎵CD 42

次の語は本文に出てくる重要語です。日本語の意味として最も適切なものを、A～Jから選んで（　）に記入しましょう。そして解答を確認した後、音声を聞いて覚えましょう。

1. useful	( )		A. 経験		
2. tool	( )		B. 役に立つ		
3. careful	( )		C. 守る		
4. protect	( )		D. 注意深い		
5. personal	( )		E. 年月日、日付		
6. date	( )		F. 道具		
7. share	( )		G. 恐ろしい、ひどい		
8. terrible	( )		H. 方法		
9. experience	( )		I. 共有する		
10. method	( )		J. 個人の		

1 **1**   These days, the Internet is a big part of our lives. It is a very useful tool for communication, entertainment, getting information, shopping, and more.

2   Of course, we must be careful and protect ourselves when we use the 5 Internet. There are some risks.

3   One of the risks on the Internet is called "**doxing**."

4   Doxing is when somebody tells everybody your personal information on the Internet.

5   Let's think of an example. You join an Internet discussion website. You 10 **post** your opinions using an **ID** (not your real name). However, somebody does not like your opinions. That person posts your name, photograph, date of birth, and other data on the website. Now everybody on the website knows your real **identity**. That is doxing.

6   But how did that person get your personal information?

15 **7**   People share a lot of information on the Internet. If you use the same ID on many websites, people can find a lot of your personal information. Social media websites, for example, have a lot of personal information. And, in some cases, people can even **hack into** your email accounts.

8   People who **are doxxed** may **be harassed** on the Internet or **in person**. It 20 can be a terrible experience.

9   But it is not difficult to protect against doxing. One simple method is to use a different ID for every website that you use.

10   Let's protect our **privacy** on the Internet!

Notes ··

doxing ドキシング（他人の個人情報をネット上にさらすこと）　**post ~** ～を投稿する　**ID** アイディー（利用者を識別するためのユーザー名のことで、「身元確認、身元証明」を意味する identification の略語）　**identity** 身元　**hack into ~** ～に不正に侵入する　**be doxxed** ドキシングされる　**be harassed** 嫌がらせを受ける（harass は「困らせる」の意味）　**in person** じかに　**privacy** プライバシー（私生活に関する情報が無断で公開されるのを避ける権利）

👥 Comprehension

本文の内容に合っていれば T を、合っていなければ F を [　] に記入しましょう。

1. [　] The Internet is useful for many things.

2. [　] If you are doxxed, people can see your personal data.

3. [　] Your personal data may include a photograph.

4. [　] Bad people might hack into your wallet.

5. [　] It is best to use the same ID for all websites.

👥 Summary

 44

次の英文は本文の要約です。1 から 8 の空所に、下の (a) ～ (h) から適語を選んで記入し文を完成させましょう。

The Internet ❶_____ us in many ways. We can access a lot of

❷_____ websites. However, there are ❸_____ on the

Internet, and one of these is called "doxing." Do you post messages on social

media? Many people do that, and most people ❹_____ their privacy

by using an ID. That is ❺_____ safe, but it is possible that a bad

person will tell everybody your real name on the Internet. They might also

❻_____ your photo and personal information such as your telephone

number. That is doxing and it is a kind of ❼_____ . People can

❽_____ your information from different websites, so always use a

different ID on every website that you use.

(a) upload	(b) protect	(c) useful	(d) usually
(e) harassment	(f) get	(g) dangers	(h) helps

🔘 Grammar Point　　　　　　　　　　助動詞

☞「動詞を助ける」と書く**助動詞**は、動詞の前に置いて様々な意味を加える働きをします。

must

A.「〜しなければならない」（必要・義務）

1. ... we **must** be careful and protect ourselves when we use the Internet. [第2段落]

B.「〜にちがいない」（推量）

2. He **must** be joking.　　彼は冗談を言っているにちがいない

can

A.「〜できる」（可能・能力）＊ 3. と 4. は「周囲の状況的に可能だ」という意味で使用されています。

3. ... people **can** find a lot of your personal information. [第7段落]

4. ... people **can** even hack into your email accounts. [第7段落]

B.「〜することがありうる」（可能性）

5. It **can** be a terrible experience. [第8段落]

may

A.「〜かもしれない」（推量）

6. People who are doxxed **may** be harassed on the Internet or in person. [第8段落]

B.「〜してもよい」（許可）

7. **May** I ask your name?　　あなたの名前を聞いてもいいですか?

should

A.「〜すべきだ」（義務・当然）

8. You **should** get up early every day.　　あなたは毎日早起きするべきだ

B.「〜のはずだ」（可能性・推量）

9. We **should** arrive there by 3 p.m.　　午後3時までにそこに着くはずだ

🔘 Grammar Practice

A. 次の日本語に合うように英文を完成させましょう。ただし、1つだけ余分な語があります。

1. 今すぐ私のオフィスに来ることができますか?

(do / you / to / come / my office / can) right now?

....

2. 図書館では大声で話すべきではありません。

(speak / should / not / you / loudly / don't) in the library.

....

3. 先生でも間違えることがあります。

(mistakes / even / make / can / must / teachers).

....

4. すぐに雨が降り始めるかもしれません。

(may / to / start / rain / it / should) soon.

....

B. 選択肢の中で最も適切なものを選んで英文を完成させましょう。

1. The baby won't stop crying. She ____ be hungry.
   (A) must not   **(B)** must   **(C)** cannot   **(D)** need

2. "Excuse me, where ____ I find a taxi?"
   (A) may   **(B)** can   **(C)** do   **(D)** am

3. If you want to pass the exam, you ____ study harder.
   (A) should   **(B)** can   **(C)** may   **(D)** will

🎧 Listening

CD 45

2人の大学生がドキシングについて話しています。会話の音声を聞いて、空欄に聞き取った英語を書き入れましょう。そして答え合わせが済んだら、パートナーと交互に役割を替えて音読練習をしてみましょう。

Lewis : Mina, do you post messages on the Internet?

Mina : Yes, [❶   ] . Why do you ask?

Lewis : Well... do you think it's [❷   ] ?

Mina : Posting messages? Yes, I think so. But we must be careful of things like doxing.

Lewis : Right. What is the best way to protect yourself, do you think?

Mina : Never post personal information, such as your home [❸   ] .

Lewis : Yeah. That's good [❹   ] .

📖 COLUMN

本文でもドキシングから身を守る方法について触れられていましたが、あるサイバーセキュリティーの会社によると、まずは自分自身について調べてみることが大切なようです。あたかも自分で自分にドキシングをするかのように、ネットで自分の個人情報を検索することによって、セキュリティーに関する様々な問題が見つかることもあるそうです。心配な人はぜひ試してみてください。

まずは「会話のヒント」について学習しましょう。その後、下の会話モデルを使って、ドキシングについて交互にインタビューをして、相手の答えを記入してください。

会話のヒント

ネットにメッセージを投稿するかどうかを聞かれたら …
Yes, often. / Yes, sometimes. / No, not so often. / No, never.

メッセージの投稿は安全だと思うかと聞かれたら …
Yes, I think it's safe. / Yes, I think it's usually safe but we must be careful./
I'm not sure. I think it might be risky.（わからない。危険かもしれない）
No, I think it's risky.

ドキシングなどの問題から身を守る方法について聞かれたら …
We must make a different ID for each website.
We should not upload personal information.
We should make good passwords and change our passwords sometimes.
（良いパスワードを作って時々変更するべきだ）

お気に入りのウェブサイトやアプリについて聞かれたら …
My favorite [website / app] is ...

A: Do you post messages on the Internet?

B: [**Response**] ....

A: I see. Do you think it's safe to post messages?

B: [**Response**] ....

A: OK. How can we protect ourselves from doxing or other problems?

B: [**Response**] ....

A: Sure. By the way, what is your favorite website or app?

B: [**Response**] ....

UNIT 12 Fast Movies

🎯 Pre-Reading Vocabulary Task

 46

次の語句は本文に出てくる重要語句です。日本語の意味として最も適切なものを、A～Jから選んで（　）に記入しましょう。そして解答を確認した後、音声を聞いて覚えましょう。

1. way	（　）		A.	方法
2. minute	（　）		B.	理由
3. illegal	（　）		C.	おそらく、たぶん
4. arrest	（　）		D.	分
5. reason	（　）		E.	主に
6. probably	（　）		F.	所属する
7. homework	（　）		G.	違法の
8. belong to	（　）		H.	逮捕する
9. mainly	（　）		I.	宿題
10. familiar	（　）		J.	おなじみの、よく知られた

1 **1** Watching movies is fun. Many people enjoy going to the **movie theater**, watching movies on TV or even watching movies on a smartphone.

2 These days there is a new way of watching movies—"**fast movies.**"

3 Fast movies **are uploaded** to **video-sharing websites**. By using **images**, 5 **moving video**, **subtitles** and **narration**, a fast movie tells the story of a movie in about 10 minutes.

4 Fast movies are illegal. In fact, the police have arrested people for making and uploading fast videos.

5 But why do some young people watch these movies?

10 **6** The first reason is probably time. College students are very busy—they have college classes and homework, they belong to clubs and circles, they might do a part-time job, and they want to **hang out with** friends. They may not have time to watch a two-hour movie.

7 Another reason is communication. When a new movie becomes 15 popular, everybody talks about it. However, if you have not seen it, it is hard to join the conversation. That can be lonely. By watching a fast movie, people can talk about it with friends.

8 Finally, on video-sharing websites and **apps**, young people mainly watch shorter **video clips**. Because a fast movie is a short clip, it is a familiar 20 **format** for young people.

9 What do you think about fast movies?

❚ Notes ❚ ....

movie theater 映画館　**fast movie** ファスト映画（映画のストーリーがわかるように短くまとめた動画）
be uploaded アップロードされる　**video-sharing website** 動画共有サイト　**image** 画像　**moving video** 動画（moving は「動いている」の意味）　**subtitle** 字幕　**narration** ナレーション　**hang out with ~** ～とぶらぶら時間を過ごす　**app** アプリ（application の略語）　**video clip** ビデオクリップ（撮影した動画の一部を切り取ったもの。clip は「切り抜き」の意味）　**format** フォーマット、形式

👥 Comprehension

本文の内容に合っていれば T を、合っていなければ F を [   ] に記入しましょう。

1. [   ] Fast movies are usually about 100 minutes long.

2. [   ] Fast movies are not legal.

3. [   ] College students have a lot of free time every day.

4. [   ] By watching a fast movie clip, people can know a movie quickly.

5. [   ] Young people tend to prefer shorter clips.

👥 Summary

 48

次の英文は本文の要約です。1 から 8 の空所に、下の (a) 〜 (h) から適語を選んで記入し文を完成させましょう。

Recently, video clips called "fast movies" have ❶ _____ . They show

movies in short versions that are usually about 10 ❷ _____ long.

Although they are ❸ _____ , some people watch them. One reason

to watch them is to ❹ _____ time. Young people are very busy, so

they may not have ❺ _____ time to watch a two-hour movie. Another

reason is to join a ❻ _____ with friends. Even if you have not seen the

❼ _____ movie, if you have seen the fast movie, you can talk about it.

Finally, in ❽ _____ , young people may prefer shorter clips.

(a) appeared	(b) enough	(c) minutes	(d) save
(e) illegal	(f) conversation	(g) general	(h) whole

🔖 Grammar Point　受動態

☞ **受動態**は〈be 動詞＋過去分詞〉の形で「～される」という意味を表します。

1. *Fast movies **are uploaded** to video-sharing websites.* ［第 3 段落］

☞ 受動態の作り方

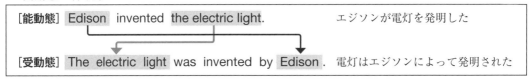

> ［能動態］ Edison　invented　the electric light.　　　エジソンが電灯を発明した
>
> ［受動態］ The electric light was invented by Edison.　電灯はエジソンによって発明された

☞ さまざまな受動態

	能動態	受動態
by 以下がない	People speak English in Ireland.	English **is spoken** in Ireland. * by people は重要な情報ではないので省略されます。
助動詞を含む	I can see the Moon.	The Moon **can be seen**.
否定文	You should not open the box.	The box **should not be opened**.
完了形	She has changed the plan.	The plan **has been changed** by her.
群動詞	He took care of the dog.	The dog **was taken care of** by him.
目的語が 2 つある （SVOO の文の場合）	She gave him the book.	He **was given** the book by her. The book **was given** (to) him by her. * 2 つの受動態を作ることができます。
目的補語がある （SVOC の文の場合）	She named the baby Alex.	The baby **was named** Alex by her. [✗] Alex was named the baby by her.
by 以外の前置詞	Snow covered our house.	Our house **was covered with** snow.
心理状態を表す	The news shocked me.	I **was shocked at** the news. * 感情を表現する時に通常、能動態は使いません。

🔖 Grammar Practice

A. 次の日本語に合うように英文を完成させましょう。ただし、1 つだけ余分な語があります。

1. 犬の赤ちゃんは英語で「パピー」と呼ばれます。

A baby dog (called / in / is / English / calls / a "puppy").

....

2. このプレゼントは私の叔父からもらいました。

I (gave / this present / was / by / my uncle / given).

....

3. その珍しい動物はその動物園では見ることができません。

The rare animal (be / in / can / see / not / seen) the zoo.

....

78

4. あのコーヒーカップは木でできているにちがいありません。

That coffee cup (by / must / of / made / wood / be).

....

B. （ ）の中の動詞または群動詞を最も適切な形に直してください。

1. The test results (tell) to her by the teacher yesterday.

2. The restaurant (close) since last Monday.

3. He (speak to) by a foreigner this morning.

Listening
CD 49

2 人の大学生がファスト映画について話しています。会話の音声を聞いて、空欄に聞き取った英語を書き入れましょう。そして答え合わせが済んだら、パートナーと交互に役割を替えて音読練習をしてみましょう。

Tomoki : Sarah, do you like movies?

Sarah : Of course! I [❶   ] them.

Tomoki : [❷   ] you ever heard of "fast movies"?

Sarah : Oh, yeah, I've heard of them.

Tomoki : What do you [❸   ] about fast movies?

Sarah : Well, I don't [❹   ] them. I like watching the real movies.

Tomoki : Yeah, me too.

📖 COLUMN

ファスト映画のことではありませんが、映画やドラマを早送りで見る若者が最近増えているという報告があります。定額制の動画配信サービスが膨大な数の作品を提供していることが、その理由の 1 つとして考えられています。いずれ音楽も早送りで聞くような時代がやって来るのでしょうか。

まずは「会話のヒント」について学習しましょう。その後、下の会話モデルを使って、ファスト映画について交互にインタビューをして、相手の答えを記入してください。

会話のヒント

映画が好きか聞かれたら …
Yes, I love them. / Yes, I like them. / They're OK. / No, not so much. / No, not at all. (まったく好きではない)

ファスト映画について聞いたことがあるかと質問されたら …
Yes, I have. / No, I haven't. / Well, I read about them in this unit.

ファスト映画についてどう思うか聞かれたら …
I think that they are [bad / not good / OK / good].

その理由を聞かれたら …
Because they are illegal.
　　　… the real movie is better. (本物の映画のほうがいいから)
　　　… they save time. (時間の節約になるから)
　　　… they help me know the movie quickly.
　　　　(その映画をすぐに知る助けになるから)

A: Do you like movies?

B: [**Response**] ....

A: Have you ever heard of fast movies?

B: [**Response**] ....

A: What do you think of fast movies?

B: [**Response**] ....

A: Why do you say that?

B: [**Response**] ....

UNIT 13
Do We Need a "Dislike" Button on Social Media?

👥 Pre-Reading Vocabulary Task

 50

次の語句は本文に出てくる重要語句です。日本語の意味として最も適切なものを、A〜Jから選んで（ ）に記入しましょう。そして解答を確認した後、音声を聞いて覚えましょう。

1. then	（　）	A．攻撃する
2. these days	（　）	B．それなら、その時
3. seem	（　）	C．まき散らす、広げる
4. cause	（　）	D．憎しみ
5. attack	（　）	E．他方で
6. spread	（　）	F．（〜するように）思われる
7. hate	（　）	G．最近
8. on the other hand	（　）	H．警告
9. warning	（　）	I．避ける
10. avoid	（　）	J．引き起こす

🔗 Reading Passage 51

1　**1**　It is fun to **post** and read messages on social media. Many people also enjoy watching **content** on **video-sharing websites and apps**.

2　If a message or video is interesting, we can **tap** the **"like" button** or the **"heart" sign**. If that message or video gets a lot of likes, then users can easily

5　find popular content.

3　But **what about** a **"dislike" button**? These days it seems that a dislike button is not an option on many services. Perhaps the dislike button is disliked.

4　Some people think that a dislike button causes problems. People might

10　**use it in a bad way**, to attack a message **poster** or content **maker**. The dislike button might be spreading hate! That is not good for the website or app.

5　On the other hand, if somebody posts terrible content, a dislike button might be useful. Seeing a lot of dislikes is a kind of warning and we can avoid that content.

15　**6**　Are there any other options? One way is to keep the dislike button but not show the dislike **count**. YouTube does this. It might stop the "dislike attacks" **mentioned above**.

7　Of course, if there is no dislike button, we can just use the number of likes as a **measure**. A lot of likes is good. Very few likes might be bad.

20　**8**　What do you think? Do you want a dislike button option?

▎Notes ▎･･･

post ～ ～を投稿する　content コンテンツ　video-sharing websites and apps 動画共有サイトやアプリ　tap ～ ～をタップする(指先で画面を軽くたたくこと)　**"like" button** 「いいね!」ボタン
"heart" sign 「ハート」マーク　what about ～ ? ～についてはどうでしょうか?　**"dislike" button**
「嫌い」ボタン　use A in a bad way A を悪用する　poster 投稿者　maker 作成者　count 総数
mentioned above 上で述べられた　measure 尺度

🌐 Comprehension

本文の内容に合っていればTを、合っていなければFを [   ] に記入しましょう。

1. [   ] The "likes" system can help us to find popular content.

2. [   ] Almost all social media services have a "dislike" button.

3. [   ] The dislike button might be used to attack people.

4. [   ] The dislike button can give us a warning of bad content.

5. [   ] The like button alone can also indicate good or bad content.

🌐 Summary

 52

次の英文は本文の要約です。1から8の空所に、下の (a) ～ (h) から適語を選んで記入し文を完成させましょう。

Social media and video-sharing services are ❶ _____ . Many people

enjoy using these websites and ❷ _____ . Many of the services have a

"like" button, ❸ _____ not so many have a "dislike" button. In fact,

some people think that a dislike button is a ❹ _____ thing. Certainly,

there are bad people who use it to attack people who post messages or

❺ _____ videos. However, other people think a dislike button can have

a ❻ _____ function. It can ❼ _____ us of bad content. Of

course, even if there is no dislike button, the number of likes alone can help us to

❽ _____ the content.

(a) warn	(b) fun	(c) apps	(d) judge
(e) useful	(f) upload	(g) but	(h) negative

☞ **形容詞**は名詞と結びついて名詞の状態や性質を説明します。それに対して、**副詞**は名詞以外のものと結びついて、場所・時・頻度・程度・様態を説明します。

1. ... *users can __easily__ find __popular__ content.* [第2段落]
   * easily は find（動詞）を修飾する副詞で、popular は content（名詞）を修飾する形容詞です。

2. *__Very few__ likes might be __bad__.* [第7段落]
   * very は few（形容詞）を修飾する副詞で、few は likes（名詞）を修飾する形容詞です。そして、bad もこの文の補語となる形容詞です。

形容詞の使い方

A. 名詞を修飾する　　　This is a **difficult** problem.　これは難しい問題だ
B. 補語になる　　　　　This problem is **difficult**.　この問題は難しい

副詞の使い方

C. 名詞以外を修飾する　This is a **very** difficult problem.　これはとても難しい問題だ
　　　　　　　　　　　This problem is **very** difficult.　この問題はとても難しい

様々な副詞の使い方

場所 （どこで）	here, near など	I want to go **abroad**. 外国に行きたい
時 （いつ）	now, then など	I went to Tokyo **yesterday**. 昨日東京に行った
頻度 （どの頻度で）	often, never など	I **always** go to school by bus. いつもバスで通学している
程度 （どの程度）	very, almost など	I can **hardly** believe him. 彼をほとんど信じられない
様態 （どのように）	well, fast など	I have to work **hard**. 一生懸命働かなければならない

間違いやすい形容詞

形容詞を動詞のあとに置いて補語として用いる（叙述用法）場合、「①人を主語にしなければならない形容詞」と「②人を主語にできない形容詞」があります。

① happy, sorry, able など
   [O] I am **glad** to hear the news.　　　[×] It is **glad** that I hear the news.
② convenient, possible, necessary など
   [O] It is **impossible** for me to dance.　　[×] I am **impossible** to dance.

🔅 Grammar Practice

A. 次の日本語に合うように英文を完成させましょう。

1. 名古屋は私のお気に入りの都市です。昨年の夏に友人とそこに行きました。
   Nagoya is my favorite city. (with / I / there / my friend / last summer / went).

....

2. 私たちは富士山をとてもはっきり見ることができました。

We were (to / Mt. Fuji / able / clearly / see / very).

....

3. 彼女は外国には住んだことがありません。

(she / abroad / lived / never / before / has).

....

4. この通りは車が非常に少ないです。

(cars / on / there / are / few / very) this street.

....

B. 選択肢の中で最も適切なものを選んで英文を完成させましょう。

1. She asked him to speak more ___ .

   (A) slow　　　**(B)** slowly　　　**(C)** slowest　　　**(D)** slower

2. "Please come when ___ ."

   (A) you're convenient　　　**(B)** it's convenient for you

   (C) you'll be convenient　　　**(D)** it's your convenient

3. It's very easy to make a salad. I have ___ finished it.

   (A) never　　　**(B)** hardly　　　**(C)** almost　　　**(D)** very

 **Listening**　　　　　　　　　　　　　　 53

2人の大学生が「いいね！」ボタンと「嫌い」ボタンについて話しています。会話の音声を聞いて、空欄に聞き取った英語を書き入れましょう。そして答え合わせが済んだら、パートナーと交互に役割を替えて音読練習をしてみましょう。

Kate　：Hey, Kento, do you watch videos on the Internet?

Kento：Sure. [❶　　　　　　　　　]. Why do you ask?

Kate　：I was thinking about the "like" and "dislike" buttons. Do you use them?

Kento：I use the [❷　　　　　　　　] button, but not the [❸　　　　　　　　] button.

Kate　：I see. Why's that?

Kento：Well, I think dislikes are a little too [❹　　　　　　　　] . If I don't like something, I don't tap like.

ある調査会社が Twitter に「嫌い」ボタンが必要かどうかをアンケートしたところ「必要だとは思わない」と答えた人が全体の約6割を占めました。一方、テレビ番組が実施した同様の調査では、両者の割合はほぼ半々という結果でした。どうやらこの問題は大きく意見の分かれる難しいテーマなのかもしれません。

👥 Speaking Pairwork

まずは「会話のヒント」について学習しましょう。その後、下の会話モデルを使って、「嫌い」ボタンについて交互にインタビューをして、相手の答えを記入してください。

会話のヒント

動画を閲覧したりソーシャルメディアを利用するか聞かれたら …
Yes, all the time.（しょっちゅう）/ Yes, often. / Yes, sometimes.

"A" や "B" を使うかどうか聞かれたら …
Yes, I use both. / I use neither.（どっちも使わない）/ I use "A" but I don't use "B."
/ I use "B" but I don't use "A."

その理由を聞かれたら …
Because it's interesting to judge content.（コンテンツを評価するのが面白いから）
　　　… I'm too lazy to use them.（使うのが面倒くさいから）
　　　… I don't like being judged, I don't want to judge other people.
　　　　（自分が評価されるのが嫌なので、他の人も評価したくない）
　　　… using the "dislike" button is too negative.
　　　　（「嫌い」ボタンを使うと過度な否定になるから）
　　　… I want to spread love by using the "like" button!
　　　　（「いいね！」ボタンを使って愛を広めたいから）

A: Do you watch videos online or use social media?

B: [**Response**] ....

A: Do you use the "like" and "dislike" buttons?

B: [**Response**] ....

A: Why's that?

B: [**Response**] ....

A: I see. By the way, can you recommend a video clip for me?

B: Sure. I recommend ....

UNIT 14

Ramen Subscription

🔹 Pre-Reading Vocabulary Task

 54

次の語は本文に出てくる重要語です。日本語の意味として最も適切なものを、A～Jから選んで（　）に記入しましょう。そして解答を確認した後、音声を聞いて覚えましょう。

1. especially	（　）		A. 混雑した
2. cost（名詞）	（　）		B. 特に
3. reasonable	（　）		C. かかる
4. offer	（　）		D. 費用
5. attractive	（　）		E. 例
6. example	（　）		F. 提供する
7. cost（動詞）	（　）		G. かなり
8. location	（　）		H. 手頃な
9. crowded	（　）		I. 場所
10. quite	（　）		J. 魅力的な

87

1 **1** **Subscription** services are popular these days. Many people use these services, especially for watching movies or listening to music.

2 There are many good points about subscriptions: they are convenient, we can access a lot of **content**, and the cost is reasonable.

5 **3** But how about for food? These days, some restaurants offer subscription options. For example, if you pay about 7,000 yen, you can eat **a bowl of** ramen every day for a month.

4 It might be an attractive offer for some people, especially people who love ramen and usually eat a lot of ramen... college students, in fact!

10 **5** How many times a month do you eat ramen at a ramen shop?

6 Let's think about the subscription example **above**. If a bowl of ramen costs about 700 yen, after just ten **visits**, you can have **free** ramen every day.

7 Therefore, if you eat ramen in a restaurant about three times a week, a ramen subscription might be a good idea.

15 **8** However, there are some things to be careful about.

9 The location of the shop is very important. It must be in a convenient place.

10 Also, the number of customers at the shop is important. If it is often crowded, it might be difficult to enter sometimes.

20 **11** Finally, some ramen shops close quite early, so we should check the **business hours**.

Notes

subscription サブスク(subscription は本来「予約購読、寄付」の意味だが、ここでは「定額料金を払って一定期間、無制限に受けられるサービス」を指す) **content** コンテンツ(ここでは主に映画や音楽といったデジタルコンテンツを指す) **a bowl of ~** 1 杯の〜 **above** 上記の(形容詞) **visit** 来店、訪問(名詞) **free** 無料の **business hours** 営業時間

👥 Comprehension

本文の内容に合っていればＴを、合っていなければＦを [　] に記入しましょう。

1. [　] Many people like to use subscription services.

2. [　] A subscription is usually very expensive.

3. [　] For 7,000 yen, you can eat three bowls of ramen every day.

4. [　] The location of the ramen shop is not so important.

5. [　] We should also check the ramen shop's closing time.

👥 Summary

 56

次の英文は本文の要約です。１から８の空所に、下の (a) 〜 (h) から適語を選んで記入し文を完成させましょう。

Many people like using subscription services to access ❶ _____ .

Recently, there are more and ❷ _____ subscriptions available. We can

even pay for a ramen subscription and eat ramen at a ramen shop every day. This

service might be a good ❸ _____ for people who eat a lot of ramen.

For ❹ _____ , if you eat ramen three times a week on average, you can

❺ _____ money with this service. But we must be ❻ _____

when choosing a ramen subscription. We should look for a shop in a convenient

location, a shop that is not too ❼ _____ and a shop that has

❽ _____ opening times.

(a) more	(b) careful	(c) idea	(d) crowded
(e) long	(f) entertainment	(g) save	(h) example

👥 Grammar Point　　　不定詞・動名詞

☞ **不定詞**は〈to +動詞の原形〉という形をとります。一方、**動名詞**は〈動詞の原形+ -ing 形〉で「〜すること」を意味します。

不定詞

1. *However, there are some things **to** be careful about.* [第 8 段落]
   * このto不定詞は形容詞用法でto be careful about が some things を修飾しています。

2. *... it might be difficult **to** enter sometimes.* [第 10 段落]
   * to enter が真の主語で it は形式主語です。

動名詞

3. *Many people use these services, especially for **watching** movies or **listening** to music.* [第 1 段落]　 * 2つの動名詞は両方とも前置詞 for の目的語になっています。

不定詞・動名詞の名詞用法

主語 **Traveling** abroad is fun. / **To travel** abroad is fun. 海外を旅するのは楽しい
補語・目的語 I like **traveling** abroad. / I like **to travel** abroad. 海外を旅するのが好きだ
前置詞の目的語 By **traveling** abroad, I can learn a lot. 海外を旅することでたくさん学べる
　　　　　 * 前置詞の後ろには動名詞しか置くことができません。

不定詞の形容詞用法

I want something **to drink**. 何か飲むものが欲しい

不定詞の副詞用法

目的（〜するために） I came here **to meet** my friend. 友人に会うためにここに来た
原因（〜して） I am so happy **to meet** you. あなたに会えてとても幸せだ

☞不定詞と動名詞で意味が異なる動詞

不定詞 I tried **to talk** to him, but I couldn't. 彼に話そうとしたができなかった
動名詞 I tried **talking** to him, but he said nothing. 試しに彼に話したが何も答えなかった
　　　　 * 不定詞の場合は「まだ話していません」が、動名詞の場合は「実際に話しています」。

👥 Grammar Practice

A. 次の日本語に合うように英文を完成させましょう。

1. 毎日英語を勉強することが重要です。
   (important / English / day / studying / is / every).

   ....

2. この公園は歩くのに良い場所です。
   This park (a / to / is / good / walk / place).

   ....

3. 彼は朝食を準備するために早く起きました。

He (prepare / got / early / to / breakfast / up).

....

4. 他の文化を理解することが必要です。

(to / it / other cultures / is / necessary / understand).

....

B. 選択肢の中で最も適切なものを選んで英文を完成させましょう。

1. I really enjoyed ___ this book.
   (A) read   (B) to read   (C) reading   (D) to reading

2. She passed the test ___ very hard.
   (A) to study   (B) by studying   (C) studying   (D) studied

3. We are looking forward ___ you again.
   (A) to meeting   (B) to meet   (C) meeting   (D) by meeting

 **Listening**   57

2人の大学生がラーメンのサブスクサービスについて話しています。会話の音声を聞いて、空欄に聞き取った英語を書き入れましょう。そして答え合わせが済んだら、パートナーと交互に役割を替えて音読練習をしてみましょう。

Emma : Hi, Takuya. What did you have for [❶   ] ?

Takuya : I had ramen at the ramen shop near the [❷   ] .

Emma : Sounds good.

Takuya : Yeah, I go there three or [❸   ] times a week.

Emma : Really? You must love it!

Takuya : I do! Actually, I have a ramen subscription for that shop.

Emma : Ah! I read about that on the Internet. Is it a good idea?

Takuya : For people who really love ramen, it's [❹   ] !

📖 COLUMN

食べ物のサブスクにもいろいろな種類があります。ラーメン以外に、大手焼肉チェーンが始めた11,000円払えば1ヵ月食べ放題になるサービス（客が殺到したため、残念ながら現在はサービス内容が変更されています）。さらに、ある大学が始めた2万円で4ヵ月間、約20種類のメニューから1日1回好きなものが食べられる「学食サブスク」などもあるようです。

 **Speaking Pairwork**

まずは「会話のヒント」について学習しましょう。その後、下の会話モデルを使って、ラーメンのサブスクサービスについて交互にインタビューをして、相手の答えを記入してください。

会話のヒント

ラーメンが好きかと聞かれたら …
I love it. / I like it. / It's OK. / I don't like it so much.

ラーメン屋でラーメンを食べる頻度を聞かれたら …
Every day. / Almost every day. / Occasionally. (時々) / Rarely. (たまに) /
Never.

ラーメンのサブスクについて聞いたことがあるかどうかを尋ねられたら …
Yes, I have. I read about it on the Internet.
　　　　　… I saw it on TV.
　　　　　… I read about it in this textbook.

ラーメンのサブスクが良いアイディアだと思うかと聞かれたら …
Yes, I do. We can save money.
　　　　　… We can have a lot of ramen.
　　　　　… It is good for people who love ramen.
No, I don't. We might eat too much ramen.
　　　　　… We might get tired of ramen. (ラーメンに飽きるかもしれない)

A: Do you like ramen?

B: [**Response**] ....

A: How often do you eat ramen in a restaurant?

B: [**Response**] ....

A: OK. Have you heard about a ramen subscription?

B: [**Response**] ....

A: Do you think it's a good idea?

B: [**Response**] ....

UNIT 15

Which Video-Sharing App Is Best?

👥 Pre-Reading Vocabulary Task

 58

次の語句は本文に出てくる重要語句です。日本語の意味として最も適切なものを、A～Jから選んで（　）に記入しましょう。そして解答を確認した後、音声を聞いて覚えましょう。

1. most	(　)	A. 作る
2. for example	(　)	B. 長さ
3. available	(　)	C. 必要な
4. both	(　)	D. 支払う
5. difference	(　)	E. 両方
6. length	(　)	F. 違い
7. create	(　)	G. 最後に
8. finally	(　)	H. 例えば
9. necessary	(　)	I. 利用できる
10. pay	(　)	J. たいていの、最も多く

93

1 **1** These days, most young people like watching videos on their smartphones.

2 A few years ago, this was not possible. The **data transfer speed** was too slow, and the limit on **gigabytes** was too low.

5 **3** But **phone networks**, smartphones and plans are much better now. We often see many young people (and older people!) watching videos while **commuting**, for example.

4 Which **video-sharing app** is the best? There are many available, but probably the two most popular apps these days are YouTube and TikTok.

10 **5** Both of these are great apps for enjoying videos. However, people seem to like them in different ways.

6 One big difference is length of videos. TikTok's **specialty** is shorter **clips**, so it is a good app for **killing time** for a few minutes. YouTube has longer videos. That is great for enjoying deeper content.

15 **7** Many of TikTok's videos **are uploaded** by ordinary young people, which means that they are fresh and **lively**. YouTube, on the other hand, has a lot of **full-time YouTubers** creating content. This means that many videos look **polished** and professional.

8 Finally, a good point about both apps is that a lot of the content is 20 **free**. It is not necessary to pay a **subscription fee**.

9 Which app do you **tend to** use most for watching videos?

Notes

----

data transfer speed データ転送速度 (transfer は「移す」の意味) **gigabyte** ギガバイト (情報量の単位) **phone network** 電話網 **commute** 通学[勤]する **video-sharing app** 動画共有アプリ **specialty** 特徴 **clip** クリップ (動画の一部を切り取ったもの) **kill time** 暇をつぶす **be uploaded** アップロードされる **lively** 元気のよい **full-time YouTuber** 専業ユーチューバー **polished** 洗練された (動詞の polish は「磨く」の意味) **free** 無料の **subscription fee** 会費 (subscription は「予約購読」の意味) **tend to do** よく…する、…する傾向がある

🔗 Comprehension

本文の内容に合っていればTを、合っていなければFを [   ] に記入しましょう。

1. [   ] These days, it is not possible to watch videos on smartphones.

2. [   ] We rarely see people watching videos on smartphones.

3. [   ] There are only two video-sharing apps.

4. [   ] Videos on TikTok tend to be longer.

5. [   ] There is a lot of free content on TikTok and YouTube.

🔗 Summary

 60

次の英文は本文の要約です。1から8の空所に、下の (a) ～ (h) から適語を選んで記入し文を完成させましょう。

Mobile networks have ❶ _____ a lot, so these days we can easily

watch videos on our smartphones. Most young people ❷ _____ videos

by using apps such as YouTube or TikTok. Both of these are ❸ _____

apps, but they are appealing in different ways. TikTok has short videos, and many

are made by ❹ _____ young people. TikTok videos are fresh and

❺ _____ . YouTube, in ❻ _____ , has many longer videos

made by experienced YouTubers. These people produce professional

❼ _____ , which is deep and polished. And, of course, an attractive

point about both TikTok and YouTube is that we can watch videos for

❽ _____ .

(a) dynamic	(b) excellent	(c) content	(d) access
(e) ordinary	(f) free	(g) improved	(h) comparison

🔵 Grammar Point　　　比較級・最上級

☞ 2つ以上のものの状態や性質などを比べる時は、形容詞や副詞を変化させて使用します。

比較級

1. *But phone networks, smartphones and plans are much __better__ now.* [第3段落]
　* 比較級の前に置かれた much は「はるかに」を意味します。

2. *TikTok's specialty is __shorter__ clips …. YouTube has __longer__ videos.* [第6段落]
　* 本文中で使用されている比較級はすべて than 以下が省略されています。

最上級　　* 4. の most の前に the をつけることもできます。

3. *Which video-sharing app is __the best__?* [第4段落]

4. *Which app do you tend to use __most__ for watching videos?* [第9段落]

☞ 比較級の3つの形

原級	as + 形容詞 / 副詞 + as …	Lisa is **as tall as** Yumi. リサはユミと同じくらいの身長だ
比較級	形容詞 / 副詞 er + than …	Kate is **taller than** Yumi. ケイトはユミより背が高い
最上級	the + 形容詞 / 副詞 est	Kate is **the tallest** of the three. 3人の中でケイトが最も背が高い

☞ 比較級・最上級の作り方

		原級	比較級	最上級
短い単語(1音節)	high(高い)		higher	highest
長い単語(3音節以上)	difficult(難しい)		more difficult	most difficult
語尾が -ly の副詞	quickly(速く)		more quickly	most quickly
不規則変化	good(よい)/ well(上手に、元気な)		better	best
不規則変化	bad(悪い)/ badly(ひどく)/ ill(病気の)		worse	worst
不規則変化	many(数が多くの)/ much(量が多くの)		more	most
不規則変化	little(量が少しの / 少し)		less	least

　* 2音節の単語は、その語によって -er,-est をつけるパターンと more, most をつけるパターンの両方があります。例えば、early は earlier, earliest で、careful は more careful, most careful です。辞書に変化の仕方が書かれているのでよく確認しましょう。

🔵 Grammar Practice

A. 次の日本語に合うように英文を完成させましょう。

1. このスーツケースはあのスーツケースと同じくらいの重さです。
　(as / this suitcase / as / is / heavy / that one).

　...

2. あなたは肉を減らして野菜を増やすべきです。
   You should (and / meat / eat / less / vegetables / more).

   ....

3. 彼女は私たちのクラスの中で一番速く走ります。
   (in / runs / she / fastest / our class / the).

   ....

4. 彼は友人よりも10分早く到着しました。
   He (than / arrived / ten / earlier / minutes / his friend).

   ....

B. 選択肢の中で最も適切なものを選んで英文を完成させましょう。

1. Unfortunately, the result of today's exam was ___ than last time.
   (A) better   (B) less   (C) worse   (D) more

2. "Which do you like ___ , cake or ice cream?"
   (A) better   (B) well   (C) worse   (D) much

3. She quit her job recently, so she spends ___ money.
   (A) better   (B) less   (C) worse   (D) more

🎧 Listening

🎵 61

2人の大学生が動画共有アプリについて話しています。会話の音声を聞いて、空欄に聞き取った英語を書き入れましょう。そして答え合わせが済んだら、パートナーと交互に役割を替えて音読練習をしてみましょう。

Natsuki : Hi, Logan. What are you [❶   ] ?

Logan　: Oh, I'm just watching a video.

Natsuki : [❷   ] app do you use to watch videos?

Logan　: I usually use TikTok. I like watching [❸   ] videos. How about you?

Natsuki : I often use YouTube.

Logan　: Cool. Why's that?

Natsuki : There are some YouTubers that I [❹   ] .

📖 COLUMN

動画共有アプリによる動画視聴が若者の生活の一部として完全に定着していることが、データの上でも明らかになりました。あるアンケート調査によると、全体の約半数が1日あたりのYouTube視聴時間を30分以内と答えたのに対し、20代だけに限ると、5人に1人が3時間以上視聴していることがわかりました。

まずは「会話のヒント」について学習しましょう。その後、下の会話モデルを使って、動画共有アプリについて交互にインタビューをして、相手の答えを記入してください。

会話のヒント

スマホでどんな動画を見るか聞かれたら …
I often watch [comedies / music videos / dance videos / joke videos / sports videos / prank videos (ドッキリ動画) / beauty videos (メイク動画) / fashion videos / animal videos / dialogues (トーク番組) / TV clips / movie clips].

よく使うアプリの使用理由を聞かれたら …
Because I prefer [shorter / longer] videos. / Because I like [動画のジャンルを入れてください]. / Because I like [ユーチューバーの名前を入れてください]. / No particular reason. (特別な理由はない)

いつ動画を見ることが多いか聞かれたら …
I tend to watch videos [on the train / at lunchtime / during break times (休み時間中に) / in the evenings].

A: What kind of videos do you watch on your smartphone?

B: [**Response**] ....

A: OK, I see. Which app do you use to watch videos?

B: [**Response**] ....

A: Cool. Why do you tend to use that app?

B: [**Response**] ....

A: That's interesting. When do you tend to watch videos?

B: [**Response**] ....

TEXT PRODUCTION STAFF

edited by Masato Kogame	編集 小亀 正人
English-language editing by Bill Benfield	英文校閲 ビル・ベンフィールド
cover design by Nobuyoshi Fujino	表紙デザイン 藤野 伸芳
text design by Nobuyoshi Fujino	本文デザイン 藤野 伸芳
DTP by ALIUS(Hiroyuki Kinouchi)	DTP アリウス（木野内 宏行）

CD PRODUCTION STAFF

| recorded by
Karen Haedrich(AmerE)
Dominic Allen(AmerE) | 吹き込み者
カレン・ヘドリック（アメリカ英語）
ドミニク・アレン（アメリカ英語） |

Trend Scope
読んで発信、社会のいま

2023年1月20日　初版発行
2024年3月10日　第4刷発行

著　　者　Jonathan Lynch
　　　　　委文　光太郎

発 行 者　佐野 英一郎

発 行 所　株式会社 成美堂
　　　　　〒101-0052　東京都千代田区神田小川町3-22
　　　　　TEL 03-3291-2261　FAX 03-3293-5490
　　　　　https://www.seibido.co.jp

印 刷・製 本　三美印刷株式会社

ISBN 978-4-7919-7265-4　　　　　　　　　Printed in Japan